LENT 2024
And My Journey
To The Cross

**Daily Mass Readings, Lenten Devotionals,
Stations of the Cross and Sacrament of Penance**

Fr. Clark T. Spencer

Published in United States of America by Catholic Lectors
Press

ISBN: 9798868459641

CONTENTS

LENT..1
Introduction..1
Lenten Practices..2
How to Use This Devotional 5
**LENT 2024 DAILY MASS READINGS AND
REFLECTIONS** 7
Wednesday, February 14 7
Thursday, February 15 9
Friday, February 16 11
Saturday, February 17..13
Sunday, February 18 15
Monday, February 19 17
Tuesday, February 20 19
Wednesday, February 21 21
Thursday, February 22...22
Friday, February 23..25
Saturday, February 24..27
Sunday, February 25 28
Monday, February 26..30
Tuesday, February 27...32
Wednesday, February 28 34
Thursday, February 29...35
Friday, March 1...37
Saturday, March 2 39
Sunday, March 3...41
Monday, March 4 43

Tuesday, March 5 44

Wednesday, March 6 46

Thursday, March 7 48

Friday, March 8 50

Saturday, March 9 51

Sunday, March 10 53

Monday, March 11 55

Tuesday, March 12 56

Wednesday, March 13 58

Thursday, March 14 60

Friday, March 15 61

Saturday, March 16 63

Sunday, March 17 65

Monday, March 18 67

Tuesday, March 19 69

Wednesday, March 20 71

Thursday, March 21 73

Friday, March 22 75

Saturday, March 23 77

Sunday, March 24 79

Monday, March 25 81

Tuesday, March 26 83

Wednesday, March 27 86

Thursday, March 28 88

Friday, March 29 90

Saturday, March 30 93

Sunday, March 31 95

STATIONS OF THE CROSS **99**

Before Each Station..99

After Each Station 99

Opening Prayer 99

First Station: Jesus in the Garden of Gethsemane................99

Second Station: Jesus, Betrayed by Judas, is Arrested.......100

Third Station: Jesus Is Condemned By the Sanhedrin 100

Fourth Station: Jesus Is Denied By Peter 101

Fifth Station: Jesus Is Judged By Pilate 102

Sixth Station: Jesus is Scourged and Crowned with Thorns102

Seventh Station: Jesus Bears The Cross 102

Eighth Station: Jesus Is Helped By Simon the Cyrenian to
Carry The Cross 103

Ninth Station: Jesus Meets the Women of Jerusalem 103

Tenth Station: Jesus Is Crucified.............................104

Eleventh Station: Jesus Promises His Kingdom to the Good
Thief..104

Twelfth Station: Jesus Speaks To His Mother and the Disciple
....105

Thirteenth Station: Jesus Dies on the Cross........................105

Fourteenth Station: Jesus Is Placed in the Tomb................105

Closing Prayer 106

SACRAMENT OF PENANCE...................................107

Examination of Conscience 107

Examination of Conscience based on the Ten
Commandments 108

Examination of Conscience based on the Precepts of the
Church 117

Confession 119

Guide to Making a Good Confession 119

Contrition 120

   Act of Contrition (traditional)..121

   Act of Contrition (alternate form).....................................121

   An Act of Contrition inspired by the Gospels....................122

   An Act of Contrition inspired by the Gospels....................122

   An Act of Contrition inspired by Psalm 51 123

   Act of Contrition inspired by Psalm 24:6-7......................123

   An Act of Contrition to Our Lord Jesus............................123

   An Act of Contrition to Jesus, the Lamb of God 123

   Act of Contrition inspired by the Prayer of Jesus 124

LENT

Introduction

Lent is one of the five seasons of the Catholic liturgical calendar, along with Advent, Christmas, Easter and Ordinary Time. It is the time of spiritual preparation prior to the Easter season, just as Advent is for Christmas. Jesus taught us clearly that there is no resurrection without the Cross, and Lent is the Church's great spiritual journey as she, the bride of Christ, joins her divine spouse in his great suffering on our behalf. The Lenten season begins on Ash Wednesday and ends approximately six weeks (40 days) later on Holy Thursday, the memorial of the Lord's Supper. The Thursday of Holy Week before Easter Sunday is known as the Holy Thursday. The last week of Lent is Holy Week, starting with Palm Sunday. Following the New Testament story, Jesus' crucifixion is commemorated on Good Friday, and at the beginning of the following week the joyful celebration of Easter Sunday recalls the Resurrection of Jesus Christ.

Lent is traditionally described as lasting for 40 days, in commemoration of the 40 days Jesus spent in the wilderness, according to the Gospels of Matthew, Mark and Luke, before beginning his public ministry, during which he fasted, prayed and endured the temptations of the devil. It is a season of penance to prepare their hearts for Easter, the greatest of all Christian feasts.

During Lent, Catholics are reminded to devote themselves to seeking the Lord in prayer, to service by giving alms, and to practice self-control through fasting. Also during Lent, the baptized are called to renew their baptismal commitment as others prepare to be baptized through the Rite of Christian Initiation of Adults, a period of learning and discernment for individuals who have declared their desire to become Catholics. The key to fruitful observance of these practices is to recognize the link to baptismal renewal. They are called not just to abstain from sin during Lent, but to true conversion of their hearts and minds as followers of Christ. They also recall those waters in which they were baptized into Christ's death, died to sin and evil, and began new life in Christ.

Lenten Practices

"The seasons and days of penance in the course of the liturgical year (Lent, and each Friday in memory of the death of the Lord) are intense moments of the Church's penitential practice. These times are particularly appropriate for: spiritual exercises, penitential liturgies, pilgrimages as signs of penance, voluntary self-denial such as fasting and almsgiving, and fraternal sharing (charitable and missionary works)." —Catechism of the Catholic Church, 1438.

Here are traditional rites Catholics practice during the Lenten season:

- **Fasting and Abstinence**

  Jesus, in Matthew's gospel, teaches us to fast: *"But when you fast, anoint your head and wash your face, so that you may not appear to others to be fasting, except to your Father who is hidden. And your Father who sees what is hidden will repay you."* (Matthew 6:17-18). Fasting is a spiritual feast. It does for the soul what food does for the body. The Bible spells out specific spiritual benefits of fasting. It produces humility (Psalm 69:10). It shows our sorrow for our sins (1 Samuel 7:6). It clears a path to God (Daniel 9:3). It is a means of discerning God's will (Ezra 8:21) and a mark of true conversion (Joel 2:12).

Ash Wednesday and Good Friday are obligatory days of fasting and abstinence for Catholics. In addition, Fridays during Lent are obligatory days of abstinence. The norms on fasting are obligatory for every Catholic from age 18 until age 59, while the norms concerning abstinence from meat are binding upon Catholics aged 14 onwards. When fasting, a person is permitted to eat one full meatless meal per day and two small meatless meals sufficient to maintain strength but do not equal a full meal. Liquids, including milk and fruit juice, are permitted. Private, self-imposed observance of fasting on Lenten weekdays and participation in daily Mass is strongly recommended. The only Catholics that are excused from fast and abstinence outside the age limits are the physically or mentally ill and this includes those individuals suffering from chronic illnesses such as diabetes. Also excluded are pregnant or nursing women. In all cases, common sense should prevail, and ill persons should not further jeopardize their health by fasting.

- **Almsgiving**

Jesus, also in Matthew's gospel, teaches us to give alms: *"But when you give alms, do not let your left hand know what your right is doing, so that your almsgiving may be secret. And your Father who sees in secret will repay you.*" (Matthew 6:3-4). Almsgiving, one of the traditional pillars of Lent, is a sign of our care for those in need and an expression of our gratitude for all that God has given to us. Works of charity and the promotion of justice are integral elements of the Christian way of life we began when we were baptized. During Lent, we are reminded to focus more intently on almsgiving, which means making the needs of others our own, especially the needy of our world. They are all around us: children and the old, the sick and the suffering, families and individuals, next-door neighbors and people in lands faraway. Whatever we give should be something of ourselves, something that costs us, as we will receive blessings from God in return. Give generously.

Generosity is not simply giving your excess clothes to a place where poor people might purchase them. It's not even writing a generous check at the time a collection is taken up for a cause that benefits the poor. These are wonderful practices, but generosity is an attitude. It is a sense that no matter how much you have, all that you have is gift, and given to you to be shared. It means that sharing with others in need should be one of your personal priorities. That is quite different from assessing all of your needs first, and then giving away what is left over. A spirit of self-less giving means that one of your needs is to share what you have with others.

Almsgiving is not only for the rich or people who have some extra spending money, but also for those who are poor or are struggling. All of us are called upon to go outside of our own personal needs and help others especially during this time, because we are always called to do this as Christians. Lent is a wonderful time to practice self-less giving, because it takes practice. It also joins us with Jesus, who gave himself completely, for us.

- **Prayer**

  Again in Matthew's gospel, Jesus teaches us to pray: *"But when you pray, go to your inner room, close the door, and pray to your Father in secret. And your Father who sees in secret will repay you."* (Matthew 6:6). Prayer is our conversation with God. Without prayer, fasting and almsgiving are merely actions we do out of tradition without much meaning. It is through prayer that we find the strength to fast. It is through prayer that we develop a closer, more intimate relationship with God. This relationship makes us so grateful for the blessings he has bestowed upon us, that we eagerly give to those less fortunate than us. We might pray especially for the grace to live out our baptismal promises more fully. We might pray for all those who will celebrate the sacrament of reconciliation with us during Lent that they will be truly renewed in their baptismal commitment.

How to Use This Devotional

This devotional is designed to accompany you through the sacred season of Lent in the year 2024. As we navigate the various themes of Lent—repentance, sacrifice, mercy, and transformation—this devotional becomes a great companion, providing daily reflections, prayers, and actions to help you draw closer to God.

Each day, we invite you to pause, reflect, and allow the Scriptures to speak into the depths of your heart. The chosen readings for each day are drawn from the rich tapestry of the Scriptures, following the liturgical calendar of the Catholic Church. Anchored in the New American Bible, Revised Edition (NABRE), these passages guide our reflections, offering timeless wisdom and insight to inspire your Lenten journey.

May this Lenten season be a time of profound encounter with the divine, a season where grace flows abundantly, and your heart is transformed by the love and mercy of our Lord Jesus Christ. May you walk this Lenten path with purpose, embracing the journey of grace that leads us to the joyous celebration of the Resurrection. Through Christ our Lord. Amen.

LENT 2024 DAILY MASS READINGS AND REFLECTIONS

First Reading: Joel 2:12-18

Responsorial Psalm: Psalm 51:3-4, 5-6ab, 12-13, 14 and 17

Second Reading: 2 Corinthians 5:20-6:2

Gospel: Matthew 6:1-6, 16-18

Reflection: A Call to Repentance and Humility

Today commemorates the beginning of Lenten season, a sacred period of reflection and spiritual renewal. The day is marked by a profound gesture—a cross of ashes upon our foreheads, a symbol of our mortality and a reminder of our need for repentance. Ashes, once the remnants of palms from the previous Palm Sunday, become a visible sign of our commitment to humble ourselves before God.

"Even now, says the LORD, return to me with your whole heart, with fasting, and weeping, and mourning." - Joel 2:12

In the First Reading, we hear the prophet's call to return to the Lord with our whole heart. This invitation to repentance is not a superficial or token gesture but a deep and profound turning toward God. Ash Wednesday is a day to confront our own imperfections, acknowledging our need for God's mercy and grace.

"A clean heart create for me, O God, and a steadfast spirit renew within me." - Psalm 51:12

The psalmist, in Psalm 51, offers a prayer for a clean heart and a steadfast spirit. As we embark on this Lenten journey, we echo this plea, seeking inner purification and unwavering resolve. Lent is an opportunity to examine our hearts, to seek forgiveness, and to cultivate a deeper relationship with the Divine.

"Behold, now is a very acceptable time; behold, now is the day of salvation." - 2 Corinthians 6:2

In St. Paul's letter to the Corinthians (Second Reading), we are reminded that now is the acceptable time and the day of salvation. The Lenten season is a favorable time for drawing nearer to God, for making amends, and for embracing the path of salvation. It is a season of transformation and renewal.

"But when you fast, anoint your head and wash your face, so that you may not appear to be fasting, except to your Father who is hidden." - Matthew 6:17-18

The Gospel of Matthew reminds us of the importance of sincerity in our Lenten practices. Fasting, prayer, and almsgiving should not be done for show but for the sake of a deeper connection with God. These practices are an intimate conversation with the Divine, a search for a heart that is open and pure.

Prayer:

Dear Heavenly Father, as we begin this Lenten journey today, we humbly approach you with contrite hearts. We recognize our need for your mercy and forgiveness. Help us to turn away from our sins and seek a deeper relationship with you. Grant us the grace to fast with sincerity, to pray with devotion, and to practice acts of charity with love in our hearts. May this season be a time of transformation and renewal as we journey toward the joy of Easter. Through Christ our Lord. Amen.

Action for the Day:

1. Attend Ash Wednesday Mass to receive ashes as a visible sign of your commitment to the Lenten journey.
2. Spend time in quiet reflection and prayer, asking God to reveal areas of your life that need repentance and transformation.
3. Consider a specific Lenten sacrifice or act of charity that you will undertake throughout this season.

Thursday, February 15

Thursday after Ash Wednesday

First Reading: Deuteronomy 30:15-20
Responsorial Psalm: Psalm 1:1-2, 3, 4 and 6
Gospel: Luke 9:22-25

Reflection: Choose Life and Follow Christ

On this second day of our Lenten journey, we reflect on the choices we make in our lives and the path we follow. The Scriptures remind us of the importance of choosing life, taking up our cross, and following Christ.

"See, I have set before you today life and prosperity, death and adversity." - Deuteronomy 30:15

In the First Reading taken from the book of Deuteronomy, Moses sets before the people of Israel a choice: life and prosperity or death and adversity. This choice is not just about physical life but also about the spiritual life that comes from obeying God's commandments. Lent is a time for us to reflect on the choices we make in our daily lives, the moral decisions that lead either toward life and blessings or death and adversity.

"Blessed is the one who does not walk in step with the wicked or stand in the way that sinners take or sit in the company of mockers." - Psalm 1:1

The Responsorial Psalm in Psalm 1 reminds us that the blessed person is one who does not walk in the ways of the wicked but delights in the law of the Lord. This Lent, let us consider our companions and the influences that shape our choices. Are we aligning ourselves with those who lead us toward God and righteousness?

"If anyone wishes to come after me, he must deny himself and take up his cross daily and follow me." - Luke 9:23

In the Gospel according to Luke, Jesus teaches that to follow Him, we must deny ourselves, take up our cross daily, and follow Him. This profound call to discipleship reminds us of the sacrifices and self-denial that are part of the Christian journey. Lent provides an opportunity for us to examine the crosses we bear and the cost of our own discipleship.

"For whoever wishes to save his life will lose it, but whoever loses his life for my sake, he is the one who will save it." - Luke 9:24

Jesus goes on to explain that those who seek to save their lives will lose them, but those who lose their lives for His sake will save them. This paradox teaches us the importance of surrender and trust in God's plan. Lent is a time to contemplate the areas in our lives where we need to let go, surrender, and entrust ourselves to the Lord.

Prayer:

Heavenly Father, as we continue our Lenten journey, we pray for the wisdom and courage to make choices that lead us closer to you. Help us to choose life and blessings over sin and adversity. May we take up our crosses daily, following your Son, Jesus Christ, and finding our lives in surrender to your divine will. Grant us the grace to embrace the paradox of losing our lives for His sake and finding true life in you. Through Christ our Lord. Amen.

Action for the Day:
1. Reflect on the choices you make in your daily life. Are they aligned with God's commandments and teachings?
2. Identify areas where you can deny yourself and take up your cross, following Jesus more closely during this Lenten season.
3. Pray for discernment in making choices that lead to spiritual growth and blessings.

Friday, February 16

Friday after Ash Wednesday

First Reading: Isaiah 58:1-9a
Responsorial Psalm: Psalm 51:3-4, 5-6ab, 18-19
Gospel: Matthew 9:14-15

Reflection: True Fasting and Acts of Compassion
Today, our reflection centers on the concept of true fasting and sincere acts of compassion. As we journey through Lent, we are reminded that our Lenten practices should go beyond external rituals to reflect a heart transformed by love and mercy.

"Is not this the fast that I choose: to loose the bonds of

wickedness, to undo the straps of the yoke, to let the oppressed go

free, and to break every yoke?" - Isaiah 58:6

In the First Reading taken from the book of Isaiah, we hear God's call for a fasting that extends beyond abstaining from food. True fasting involves breaking the bonds of wickedness, relieving the oppressed, and setting people free. It is a fasting that embodies justice, compassion, and love for one's neighbor.

"For I desire steadfast love and not sacrifice, the knowledge of

God rather than burnt offerings." - Hosea 6:6

God desires steadfast love and knowledge of Him more than external sacrifices and rituals. This Lent, we are called to prioritize our relationship with God, deepening our knowledge of Him and living out His love in our interactions with others.

"Can the wedding guests mourn as long as the bridegroom is

with them? The days will come when the bridegroom is taken

away from them, and then they will fast." - Matthew 9:15

In the Gospel of Matthew, Jesus speaks about fasting in the context of His presence. He refers to Himself as the bridegroom, and His disciples do not fast while He is with them. However, He foreshadows a time of fasting when He will be taken away. This season of Lent is that time of fasting, a time for us to seek God more intensely and prepare for His coming.

Prayer:

Heavenly Father, on this Friday of Lent, we are reminded of the significance of true fasting/abstinence and acts of compassion. Help us to look beyond external rituals and seek the transformation of our hearts. Grant us the grace to break the bonds of wickedness, to relieve the oppressed, and to set the captives free. May our fasting/abstinence and Lenten practices be an outpouring of love and mercy to those in need. Through Christ our Lord. Amen.

Action for the Day:
1. Be reminded of the tradition of abstaining from meat on Fridays during Lent and if possible fast.
2. Consider how your Lenten practices can extend beyond personal sacrifice to benefit those in need. Identify opportunities to show compassion and alleviate suffering in your community or among your acquaintances.
3. Reflect on how you can prioritize your relationship with God and grow in the knowledge of His love during this Lenten season.

Saturday, February 17

Saturday after Ash Wednesday

First Reading: Isaiah 58:9b-14
Responsorial Psalm: Psalm 86:1-2, 3-4, 5-6
Gospel: Luke 5:27-32

Reflection: Responding to God's Call
In the journey to the cross, there will be a lot of obstacles to deter us from receiving the grace of God especially in this Lenten season. Today, we reflect on God's call to us, just as Jesus called Matthew, the tax collector, to follow Him. This day is an opportunity for us to leave behind our old ways and embrace the path of discipleship.

"If you remove the yoke from your midst, the pointing of the finger, and speaking wickedness, if you give yourself to the hungry and satisfy the desire of the afflicted, then your light will rise in darkness and your gloom will become like midday." -
Isaiah 58:9b-10

In the book of Isaiah, we are reminded that true repentance involves not only personal change but also a change in how we treat others. When we remove oppression and extend compassion to those in need, our lives are illuminated by God's grace. This Lent, we are called to let go of judgment and embrace a spirit of love and charity.

"Incline your ear, O Lord, and answer me, for I am poor and needy." - Psalm 86:1

The psalmist's cry for God's response resonates with our longing for God's guidance and presence during Lent. We acknowledge our poverty and neediness and turn to the Lord for His mercy and direction.

"Those who are well have no need of a physician, but those who are sick. I have not come to call the righteous but sinners to repentance." - Luke 5:31-32

In the Gospel of Luke, we witness Jesus calling Matthew, a tax collector and sinner, to follow Him. Jesus' mission is to call sinners to repentance, to offer healing to the spiritually sick. During Lent, we remember that we are all in need of God's healing and grace.

Prayer:

Heavenly Father, today, we respond to your call to follow your Son, Jesus Christ. We acknowledge our need for your mercy and recognize that we are all in need of repentance. Help us to remove the yoke of judgment and to extend compassion to those who are hungry and afflicted. May we be obedient to your call and willing to leave behind our old ways, embracing the path of discipleship. Through Christ our Lord. Amen.

Action for the Day:

1. Reflect on your own call to discipleship. In what ways is God calling you to follow Him more closely during this Lenten season?
2. Consider how you can extend compassion and charity to those in need, both spiritually and materially.
3. Spend time in prayer, seeking God's guidance and presence in your life.

Sunday, February 18

First Sunday of Lent

First Reading: Genesis 9:8-15

Responsorial Psalm: Psalm 25:4-5, 6-7, 8-9

Second Reading: 1 Peter 3:18-22

Gospel: Mark 1:12-15

Reflection: Facing Temptation and Embracing the Gospel

On this First Sunday of Lent, we find ourselves at the beginning of Jesus' public ministry. It's a day to reflect on His time in the desert, where He faced temptation and began His mission, as well as the invitation to repent and embrace the Gospel.

"And a voice came from heaven, 'You are my beloved Son; with

you I am well pleased.'" - Mark 1:11

Before facing temptation in the wilderness, Jesus received affirmation from God, His Father. It's a reminder of His beloved status and the approval of His mission. As we begin our Lenten journey, may we too remember our *belovedness* in the eyes of God.

"And the Spirit immediately drove him out into the wilderness." - Mark 1:12

The Holy Spirit led Jesus into the wilderness, where He fasted for 40 days and faced temptation from the devil. Lent, likewise, is a time for us to be led by the Spirit into self-examination and spiritual growth, confronting the temptations that challenge our faith.

"Repent and believe in the gospel." - Mark 1:15

In the Gospel of Mark, Jesus proclaims the arrival of the Kingdom of God and calls people to repent and believe in the gospel. This call is at the heart of Lent—a time to turn away from sin and embrace the good news of salvation.

"Baptism, which corresponds to this, now saves you, not as a removal of dirt from the body but as an appeal to God for a good conscience, through the resurrection of Jesus Christ." - 1 Peter 3:21

Peter's letter in the Second Reading emphasizes the significance of baptism as a symbol of cleansing and an appeal to God for a good conscience. During Lent, we reflect on our own baptismal promises and the renewal of our commitment to follow Christ.

Prayer:

Heavenly Father, on this First Sunday of Lent, we reflect on Jesus' time in the desert, His confrontation with temptation, and His proclamation of the Gospel. Help us to remember our *belovedness* as your children and to face our own temptations with strength and faith. May we heed the call to repent and believe in the Gospel, turning away from sin and embracing the good news of salvation. As we journey through this season, grant us the grace to renew our baptismal promises and draw nearer to you. Through Christ our Lord. Amen.

Action for the Day:

1. Reflect on your baptismal promises and consider how you can renew your commitment to follow Christ during Lent.
2. Spend time in prayer and self-examination, identifying areas of temptation or sin in your life that you wish to confront and overcome. Go for confession in order to receive the abundant grace of God through Jesus Christ.
3. Consider how you can proclaim the gospel in your daily life, both through your words and actions.

Monday, February 19

Monday of the First Week of Lent

First Reading: Leviticus 19:1-2, 11-18
Responsorial Psalm: Psalm 19:8, 9, 10, 15
Gospel: Matthew 25:31-46

Reflection: Practicing Love and Charity

On this Monday of the first week of Lent, our reflection centers on the theme of love and charity, as we explore how to practice these virtues in our daily lives. The readings guide us to understand the importance of loving our neighbors and showing charity to those in need.

"You shall love your neighbor as yourself. I am the LORD." -
Leviticus 19:18

In the Second Reading taken from the book of Leviticus, we find the command to love our neighbors as ourselves. This principle is at the core of ethical living and is central to the teachings of Christ. It is a call to treat others with the same love, compassion, and respect that we desire for ourselves.

"The judgments of the LORD are true and righteous altogether.
More to be desired are they than gold, even much fine gold;
sweeter also than honey, and drippings of the honeycomb." -
Psalm 19:9-10

Psalm 19 reflects on the desirability and beauty of God's judgments, likening them to precious gold and the sweetness of honey. This perspective encourages us to see God's guidance as a source of wisdom and righteousness that we should cherish.

"Truly, I say to you, as you did it to one of the least of these my
brothers, you did it to me." - Matthew 25:40

In the Gospel of Matthew, Jesus teaches that acts of charity to those in need are acts of service to Him. This message underscores the importance of extending love and help to the marginalized and suffering, as we find Christ in them.

Prayer:

Heavenly Father, on this Monday of Lent, we reflect on the call to love our neighbors as ourselves. Help us to embody this commandment in our daily lives, showing kindness, compassion, and charity to those around us. Open our hearts to recognize your presence in the least of these, so that our acts of love become acts of service to you. Grant us the grace to see the beauty of your guidance and the desirability of your righteous judgments. Through Christ our Lord. Amen.

Action for the Day:

1. Identify one way you can practice love and charity towards your neighbors today.
2. Reflect on how your actions toward others reflect your love for God.
3. Consider seeking out opportunities for acts of charity and kindness during this Lenten season.

Tuesday, February 20

Tuesday of the First Week of Lent

First Reading: Isaiah 55:10-11

Responsorial Psalm: Psalm 34:4-5, 6-7, 16-17, 18-19

Gospel: Matthew 6:7-15

Reflection: The Power of Prayer and Forgiveness

On this Tuesday of the first week of Lent, our reflection centers on the power of prayer and forgiveness. The readings remind us of the significance of both in our spiritual journey.

"For as the rain and the snow come down from heaven and do not return there but water the earth, making it bring forth and sprout, giving seed to the sower and bread to the eater." - Isaiah

55:10

Prophet Isaiah's imagery of rain and snow from heaven nurturing the earth reminds us of God's word and His providence. Just as rain and snow bring life to the earth, God's word nurtures our souls. Prayer is a means by which we receive and internalize this divine nourishment.

"The eyes of the LORD are toward the righteous and his ears toward their cry." - Psalm 34:15

The psalmist reassures us that God's attention is directed toward the righteous and that He listens to their cries. In our prayers, we have the privilege of direct communication with the Divine, knowing that God hears and responds to our heartfelt supplications.

"For if you forgive others their trespasses, your heavenly Father will also forgive you." - Matthew 6:14

In the Gospel of Matthew, Jesus emphasizes the importance of forgiveness in our prayer life. Forgiving others is a condition for receiving forgiveness from God. Lent is an ideal time to examine our hearts and practice forgiveness towards those who have wronged us.

Prayer:

Heavenly Father, on this Tuesday of Lent, we are reminded of the power of prayer and the importance of forgiveness. We thank you for the nourishment of your word and the assurance that you hear our cries. Help us to approach you in prayer with sincerity and humility. Grant us the grace to forgive as we have been forgiven, freeing our hearts from the burden of resentment and anger. May our Lenten journey be marked by a deeper understanding of the transformative power of prayer and forgiveness. Through Christ our Lord. Amen.

Action for the Day:

1. Spend time in prayer, lifting up your needs and the needs of others to God.
2. Reflect on any unresolved conflicts or grudges in your life, and consider taking steps toward forgiveness.
3. Practice the Lord's Prayer as a model of effective and heartfelt prayer.

Wednesday, February 21

Wednesday of the First Week of Lent

First Reading: Jonah 3:1-10
Responsorial Psalm: Psalm 51:3-4, 12-13, 18-19
Gospel: Luke 11:29-32

Reflection: Responding to God's Call with Repentance

On this Wednesday of the first week of Lent, our reflection centers on the story of Jonah, the call to repentance, and the response to God's call. Jonah's journey serves as a reminder of our own need for repentance and obedience to God's will.

"The word of the Lord came to Jonah a second time." - Jonah 3:1

In the book of Jonah, we see that God's call came to Jonah a second time after his initial reluctance and disobedience. God is patient and persistent in calling us to repentance and faith, even when we stray.

"A broken and contrite heart, O God, you will not despise." -
Psalm 51:17

Psalm 51 speaks of the value of a broken and contrite heart in God's eyes. During Lent, we are called to approach God with humility, acknowledging our need for repentance and His mercy.

"This generation is an evil generation; it seeks a sign, but no sign will be given it, except the sign of Jonah." - Luke 11:29

In the Gospel of Luke, Jesus speaks of the sign of Jonah as a symbol of repentance. Just as Jonah spent three days in the belly of the fish, Jesus would spend three days in the heart of the earth. This is a sign of transformation and rebirth, a call to turn our hearts toward God and seek His mercy.

Prayer:

Heavenly Father, on this Wednesday of Lent, we reflect on the story of Jonah and the call to repentance. We are grateful for your patience and persistent love that calls us back to you. Help us to respond to your call with a contrite heart, acknowledging our need for your mercy and grace. May the sign of Jonah and the three days in the heart of the earth remind us of the transformative power of repentance and the promise of rebirth in Christ. Through Christ our Lord. Amen.

Action for the Day:

1. Reflect on areas of your life where you need to turn back to God in repentance.

2. Consider ways in which you can respond to God's call and align your life with His will during this Lenten season.

3. Catechumens who have been preparing for baptism will soon be initiated into the Church. Say a prayer for all the elect, whose journeys of spiritual growth have led them to

becoming our brothers and sisters in Christ.

First Reading: 1 Peter 5:1-4
Responsorial Psalm: Psalm 23:1-3a, 4, 5, 6
Gospel: Matthew 16:13-19

Reflection: You are the Christ, the son of the living God
On this Thursday of the first week of Lent, we celebrate the Feast of the Chair of St. Peter the Apostle, celebrating the Primacy and Authority of St. Peter as the Vicar of Christ and the representative of the Head of the Church, Our Lord Jesus Christ. Today we focus our attention on the centrality of the role of St. Peter and his successors, the Popes, in the governance and leadership of the entire Church. The readings guide us to understand the importance of serving people willingly, eagerly and unselfishly, and also the recognition of Christ's identity. Just as Peter declared Jesus as the Christ and was entrusted with leadership, may we too embrace our roles in shepherding others and proclaiming the Gospel.

"Tend the flock of God in your midst, [overseeing] not by constraint but willingly, as God would have it, not for shameful profit but eagerly." - 1 Peter 5:2

In the first reading, Peter, the Apostle, exhorts the presbyters (officially appointed leaders and teachers of the Christian community) to shepherd the flock with humility, imitating the

23

Chief Shepherd, Jesus Christ. As we embark on the Lenten journey, let us consider our roles as shepherds, guiding others with the love and humility exemplified by Christ.

"The LORD is my shepherd; there is nothing I lack." - Psalm 23:1

The Shepherd's Psalm reassures us of God's tender care, guiding us through the Lenten season and beyond. Let us find solace in the Lord's presence, trusting in His guidance and provision.

"Simon Peter said in reply, 'You are the Messiah, the Son of the living God.'" - Matthew 16:16

In today's Gospel, Jesus questions His disciples about His identity, and Peter declares Him as the Christ, the Son of the living God. In response, Jesus gives Peter the keys of the kingdom, signifying his role in the leadership of the Church. As we reflect on this Gospel passage, let us acknowledge Jesus as our Lord and Savior and recognize the authority given to Peter.

Prayer:

Heavenly Father, as we celebrate the Feast of the Chair of Saint Peter during this Lenten season, we are reminded of the importance of humility and servant leadership. Grant us the grace to shepherd your flock with care and humility, recognizing Jesus as the Christ and acknowledging the authority entrusted to Peter. May we follow in the footsteps of the Good Shepherd, finding solace in your guidance. Through Christ our Lord. Amen.

Action for the Day:

1. Spend time in prayer, asking for the grace to shepherd others with love and humility.
2. Reflect on areas where pride or self-sufficiency may be

hindering your ability to seek God's guidance.

3. Reflect on Psalm 23, seeking comfort in the Lord's shepherding care throughout the Lenten journey.

4. In honor of St. Peter, our first pope, say a prayer for priests today.

Friday, February 23

Friday of the First Week of Lent

First Reading: Ezekiel 18:21-28

Responsorial Psalm: Psalm 130:1-2, 3-4, 5-7a, 7bc-8

Gospel: Matthew 5:20-26

Reflection: Reconciliation and Acts of Mercy

On this Friday of the first week of Lent, our reflection centers on the themes of reconciliation and acts of mercy. The readings guide us to understand the importance of forgiveness, repentance, and reconciliation in our spiritual journey.

"But if the wicked person turns away from all the sins they have committed and keeps all my decrees and does what is just and right, that person will surely live; they will not die." - Ezekiel 18:21

In today's First Reading, we find the promise of life and salvation for those who turn away from sin, keeping God's decrees, and doing what is just and right. This message emphasizes the opportunity for repentance and transformation.

"If you, LORD, kept a record of sins, Lord, who could stand? But with you there is forgiveness, so that we can, with reverence, serve you." - Psalm 130:3-4

25

The psalmist acknowledges God's forgiveness and mercy. It is a reminder that our God is a forgiving God who offers us the opportunity to turn to Him with repentant hearts. Lent is a time to recognize our need for God's forgiveness and to revere Him through our service.

"So if you are offering your gift at the altar and there remember that your brother or sister has something against you, leave your gift there before the altar and go. First be reconciled to your brother or sister, and then come and offer your gift." - Matthew 5:23-24

In today's Gospel, Jesus teaches the importance of reconciliation and the priority of mending broken relationships. Our acts of worship and devotion are to be preceded by acts of reconciliation and forgiveness. This underscores the value of peacemaking in our journey of faith.

Prayer:

Heavenly Father, on this Friday of Lent, we reflect on the themes of reconciliation and acts of mercy. We are grateful for the promise of life and salvation when we turn away from sin and seek to do what is just and right. Help us to recognize the depth of your forgiveness and the importance of reconciling with others. Grant us the grace to be peacemakers and to offer our worship with hearts that are free from animosity and conflict. May our Lenten journey be marked by a spirit of reconciliation and acts of mercy. Through Christ our Lord. Amen.

Action for the Day:

1. Reflect on your relationships and consider whether there

are any conflicts or grievances that need to be addressed. Also make going to confession a priority during this Lenten season.

2. Reach out to someone with whom you may have unresolved issues and take a step toward reconciliation and forgiveness.

3. Seek opportunities to show acts of mercy and kindness to those in need.

Saturday, February 24
Saturday of the First Week of Lent

First Reading: Deuteronomy 26:16-19
Responsorial Psalm: Psalm 119:1-2, 4-5, 7-8
Gospel: Matthew 5:43-48

Reflection: Loving Your Enemies

On this Saturday of the first week of Lent, our reflection centers on the challenging call to love our enemies, as Jesus teaches in the Gospel of Matthew. This call challenges us to strive for a love that transcends human limitations.

"You shall be holy, for I the LORD your God am holy." - Deuteronomy 26:19

In the First Reading from the book of Deuteronomy, we find a call to holiness. God's people are called to imitate the holiness of God, who is perfect in love and justice. This call to holiness sets the foundation for the challenging teaching of Jesus.

"Blessed are they who observe his decrees, who seek him with all their heart." - Psalm 119:2

The psalmist recognizes the blessings that come from seeking God and observing His decrees. Loving our enemies is a manifestation of God's command to love one another, and it's an act of obedience that brings blessings.

"You have heard that it was said, 'you shall love your neighbor and hate your enemy.' But I say to you, love your enemies, and pray for those who persecute you, that you may be children of your heavenly Father." - Matthew 5:43-45

In today's Gospel of Matthew, Jesus challenges the conventional wisdom of loving only our neighbors and teaches that true disciples are called to love even their enemies. This love is a reflection of God's love for all, and it is a sign of being children of our heavenly Father.

Prayer:

Heavenly Father, on this Saturday of Lent, we reflect on the profound teaching of Jesus to love our enemies. We acknowledge the challenge of this command but recognize that it is an expression of your divine love and holiness. Grant us the grace to love those who oppose us, to pray for those who persecute us, and to be children of our heavenly Father. May our Lenten journey be marked by a deepening of love and a willingness to live out the radical love taught by your son. Through Christ our Lord. Amen.

Action for the Day:

1. Reflect on anyone you may consider an "enemy" or someone who hurt you and broke your trust.
2. Consider how you can extend love and prayers to that person, seeking reconciliation and understanding.

3. Pray for the grace to embody the love of Christ, even in the face of opposition.

First Reading: Genesis 22:1-2, 9a, 10-13, 15-18
Responsorial Psalm: Psalm 116:10, 15, 16-17, 18-19
Second Reading: Romans 8:31b-34
Gospel: Mark 9:2-10

Reflection: Trust and Obedience

On this Second Sunday of Lent, we find ourselves in the presence of two profound narratives that encourage us to reflect on trust and obedience in our journey of faith.

"Here I am." - Genesis 22:1

The story of Abraham's willingness to offer his son Isaac as a sacrifice begins with his response, "Here I am." It symbolizes a willingness to listen to God's call and to trust in His plan. Abraham's obedience, even in the face of a seemingly impossible request, demonstrates unwavering faith and trust in God's providence.

"I believed, even when I said, 'I am greatly afflicted.'" - Psalm 116:10

The psalmist's words reflect the idea that even in times of great affliction, trust in God remains steadfast. It's a reminder that our trust in God is not solely dependent on circumstances but grounded in our belief in His faithfulness.

"If God is for us, who can be against us?" - Romans 8:31

In his letter to the Romans in the Second Reading, Paul emphasizes the security that comes from God's love and presence. This assurance of God being for us gives us the strength to trust Him in all circumstances.

"This is my beloved Son. Listen to him." - Mark 9:7

During the transfiguration of Jesus, God the Father affirms Jesus as His beloved Son and instructs the disciples to listen to Him. This moment underscores the significance of trusting in Jesus as our Lord and Savior and being obedient to His teachings.

Prayer:

Heavenly Father, on this Second Sunday of Lent, we reflect on the themes of trust and obedience in the face of challenges and difficulties. We acknowledge the deep trust demonstrated by Abraham and the unwavering faith of the psalmist. Grant us the grace to trust in your providence, even in the midst of affliction, and to be obedient to your son, Jesus Christ, as our Lord and Savior. May our Lenten journey be marked by a deepening of trust and a commitment to listen to your word. Through Christ our Lord. Amen.

Action for the Day:

1. Reflect on areas in your life where trust and obedience to God may be tested or strengthened.
2. Consider how you can deepen your trust in God's providence and be more obedient to His teachings.
3. Spend time in prayer and scripture, listening to the guidance of Jesus in your life.

First Reading: Daniel 9:4b-10

Responsorial Psalm: Psalm 79:8, 9, 11 and 13

Gospel: Luke 6:36-38

Reflection: Forgiveness and Mercy

On this Monday of the Second Week of Lent, the readings invite us to engage in sincere self-reflection and seek God's mercy. The prayer of Daniel, the plea for compassion in the psalm, and the call to be merciful in the Gospel all align to guide us on a path of repentance and generosity.

"O LORD, we are ashamed, like our kings, our princes, and our ancestors, for having sinned against you." - Daniel 9:8

In the first reading, Daniel offers a prayer of repentance and acknowledges the sins of the people. As we enter the second week of Lent, let us also reflect on our shortcomings, seeking God's mercy and grace.

"Help us, God our savior, on account of the glory of your name.

Deliver us, pardon our sins for your name's sake." - Psalm 79:9

The psalmist implores God's compassion and forgiveness for the sins of the people. During Lent, let us turn to the Lord with contrite hearts, trusting in His mercy to restore and renew us.

"Be merciful, just as [also] your Father is merciful." - Luke 6:36

In today's Gospel, Jesus instructs His disciples to be merciful, just as the Father is merciful. He emphasizes the principle of giving and receiving, encouraging generosity and forgiveness. As we meditate on this Gospel, let us consider how we can embody God's mercy in our interactions with others.

Prayer:

Heavenly Father, as we journey through the second week of Lent, we acknowledge our sins and shortcomings. Like Daniel, we turn to you in repentance, seeking your mercy and forgiveness. Grant us the grace to be instruments of your mercy in our interactions with others. May our hearts be open to giving generously, knowing that we, too, receive abundantly from your loving hand. Through Christ our Lord. Amen.

Action for the Day:

1. Take time for personal reflection, acknowledging areas where you need God's mercy.
2. Pray the psalm as a personal plea for God's compassion and forgiveness.
3. Look for opportunities to practice mercy and generosity in your interactions with others.

Tuesday, February 27

Tuesday of the Second Week of Lent

First Reading: Isaiah 1:10, 16-20

Responsorial Psalm: Psalm 50:8-9, 16bc-17, 21 and 23

Gospel: Matthew 23:1-12

Reflection: Authentic Faith and Humility

On this Tuesday of the second week of Lent, our reflection centers on the importance of authentic faith and humility. The readings guide us to understand the significance of sincerity in our relationship with God.

"Wash yourselves; make yourselves clean; remove the evil of your deeds from before my eyes; cease to do evil." - Isaiah 1:16

The passage from Isaiah calls for self-examination and purification. God desires sincere repentance and a turning away from evil deeds as a sign of authentic faith.

"Offer to God a sacrifice of thanksgiving and perform your vows to the Most High, and call upon me in the day of trouble; I will deliver you, and you shall glorify me." - Psalm 50:14-15

The psalmist emphasizes the importance of offering thanksgiving and fulfilling vows to God. This expresses a genuine relationship with God, grounded in gratitude and trust.

"The greatest among you must be your servant. Whoever exalts himself will be humbled, but whoever humbles himself will be exalted." - Matthew 23:11-12

In today's Gospel of Matthew, Jesus teaches about the humility that should characterize His followers. True greatness, in the eyes of God, lies in servanthood and humility, rather than seeking exaltation.

Prayer:

Heavenly Father, on this Tuesday of Lent, we reflect on the themes of authentic faith and humility. We acknowledge the importance of genuine repentance, gratitude, and service in our relationship with you. Help us to cleanse ourselves from evil deeds, to offer thanksgiving, and to humbly serve others. May our Lenten journey be marked by an authentic and humble faith, glorifying you in all that we do. Through Christ our Lord. Amen.

Action for the Day:

1. Reflect on areas in your life where authenticity in your faith may need improvement.
2. Consider how you can express gratitude to God and fulfill any vows or commitments you've made to Him.
3. Look for opportunities to serve others with humility and sincerity rather than with pride and self-exaltation.

Wednesday, February 28

Wednesday of the Second Week of Lent

First Reading: Jeremiah 18:18-20

Responsorial Psalm: Psalm 31:5-6, 14, 15-16

Gospel: Matthew 20:17-28

Reflection: Service and Selflessness

On this Wednesday of the second week of Lent, our reflection centers on the themes of service and selflessness. The readings guide us to understand the importance of humility and serving others as we follow the example set by Jesus.

"Come, let us contrive a plot against Jeremiah. It will not mean the loss of instruction from the priests, nor of counsel from the wise, nor of messages from the prophets." - Jeremiah 18:18

The passage from Jeremiah in the First Reading highlights the resistance and plotting against the prophet. It serves as a reminder that the world may sometimes oppose those who bring God's message of truth and justice.

"Into your hands, I commend my spirit." - Psalm 31:5

The psalmist expresses complete trust in God by commending their spirit into His hands. This act of surrender and reliance on God is a demonstration of humility and selflessness.

"Whoever wishes to be great among you shall be your servant; whoever wishes to be first among you shall be your slave." -

Matthew 20:26-27

In today's Gospel of Matthew, Jesus teaches His disciples about true greatness. He emphasizes the importance of serving others and being a servant. Selflessness and a willingness to put others first are qualities that reflect His teachings.

Prayer:

Heavenly Father, on this Wednesday of Lent, we reflect on the themes of service and selflessness. We acknowledge the opposition and challenges that may arise when we seek to follow your path of truth and justice. Help us to trust in you completely and to commend our spirits into your hands. Grant us the grace to be true servants, putting others before ourselves and aspiring to greatness through selflessness. May our Lenten journey be marked by a humble and servant-hearted faith, following the example set by Your Son, Jesus Christ. Through Christ our Lord. Amen.

Action for the Day:

1. Reflect on how you can be of service to others, especially in situations where you can put others' needs ahead of your own.

2. Practice selflessness by taking on a humble and servant-hearted attitude in your interactions with others.

3. Spend time in prayer, surrendering your cares and

concerns into God's loving hands.

First Reading: Jeremiah 17:5-10

Responsorial Psalm: Psalm 1:1-2, 3, 4 and 6

Gospel: Luke 16:19-31

Reflection: Roots of Faith and the Call to Mercy

On this Thursday of the Second Week of Lent, the Scriptures invite us to reflect on the roots of our faith, the blessings that come from trusting in God, and the call to mercy and compassion.

"Blessed are those who trust in the Lord, whose trust is the Lord. They shall be like a tree planted by water, sending out its roots by the stream." - Jeremiah 17:7-8

Jeremiah's words paint a vivid picture of the blessings that come from trusting in the Lord. Like a tree planted by water, those who trust in God find stability, nourishment, and a continual source of life. As we journey through Lent, may our trust in God deepen, and may our lives be firmly rooted in His grace.

"Blessed are they who hope in the Lord." - Psalm 1:3

The psalmist echoes the theme of trust and hope in the Lord, portraying the blessedness of those who find their refuge in Him. In a world filled with uncertainties, our hope in God becomes an anchor for the soul, providing strength and assurance.

"There was a rich man who was dressed in purple and fine linen and who feasted sumptuously every day. And at his gate lay a poor man named Lazarus, covered with sores..." - Luke 16:19-20

36

In today's Gospel of Luke, Jesus tells a parable highlighting the stark contrast between a wealthy man and a poor beggar named Lazarus. Despite the rich man's material abundance, he fails to show mercy to Lazarus, who is in desperate need. This parable challenges us to examine our hearts and respond to the call of mercy and compassion.

Prayer:

Heavenly Father, on this Thursday of the Second Week of Lent, we contemplate the importance of trust, hope, and mercy in our lives. Like a tree planted by water, may our roots of faith go deep, drawing sustenance from your grace. Help us to place our trust and hope in you, finding stability and strength in the midst of life's challenges. As we encounter the parable of the rich man and Lazarus, open our hearts to the call of mercy, that we may extend compassion to those in need. Through Christ our Lord. Amen.

Action for the Day:

1. Reflect on the areas of your life where you need to deepen your trust in God.
2. Consider how you can be a source of hope and mercy to those around you, especially those who may be in need.
3. Spend time in prayer, thanking God for His faithfulness and seeking guidance on how to live a life rooted in trust and mercy.

Friday, March 1

Friday of the Second Week of Lent

First Reading: Genesis 37:3-4, 12-13a, 17b-28a

Responsorial Psalm: Psalm 105:16-17, 18-19, 20-21

Gospel: Matthew 21:33-43, 45-46

Reflection: God's Providence and Our Response

On this Friday of the second week of Lent, our reflection centers on the idea of God's providence and our response to His guidance. The readings guide us to understand the importance of recognizing God's providential care and aligning our lives with His will.

"But they hated him and could not speak peaceably to him." -
Genesis 37:4

The story of Joseph and his brothers in Genesis highlights the hatred and jealousy that arose among his siblings. Despite this, God's providential plan was at work, ultimately leading to Joseph's role in saving his family.

"When there was a famine in the land and severe hardship, our
ancestors could find nothing to eat." - Psalm 105:16

The psalmist recalls the hardships faced by their ancestors, emphasizing the significance of God's intervention and providence during times of need.

"The stone that the builders rejected has become the cornerstone;
by the Lord has this been done, and it is wonderful in our eyes." -
Matthew 21:42

In the Gospel of Matthew, Jesus references the stone that the builders rejected, which has become the cornerstone. This stone represents Jesus Himself, the foundation of God's providential plan for salvation.

Prayer:

Heavenly Father, on this Friday of Lent, we reflect on the themes of your providence and our response to your guidance. We recognize the challenges and hardships faced by our ancestors and your hand in providing for them. Help us to see your providence at work in our own lives, even in the midst of difficulties. May we align our lives with your will and acknowledge Jesus as the cornerstone of our faith. Grant us the grace to trust in your plan, even when it may be difficult to understand. May our Lenten journey be marked by a deeper awareness of your providence and a willingness to follow your guidance. Through Christ our Lord. Amen.

Action for the Day:

1. Reflect on moments in your life where you've witnessed God's providential care, even in challenging times.
2. Spend time in prayer, thanking God for His providence and seeking His guidance for your life.
3. Be reminded that the norms concerning abstinence from meat are binding upon all Catholics from age 14 onward.

Saturday, March 2

Saturday of the Second Week of Lent

First Reading: Micah 7:14-15, 18-20
Responsorial Psalm: Psalm 103:1-2, 3-4, 9-10, 11-12
Gospel: Luke 15:1-3, 11-32

Reflection: God's Forgiveness and Mercy

On this Saturday of the second week of Lent, our reflection centers on the themes of God's forgiveness and mercy. The readings guide us to understand the boundless love and compassion of our Heavenly Father.

"Who is there like you, the God who removes guilt and pardons sin for the remnant of his inheritance; Who does not persist in anger forever, but delights rather in clemency?" - Micah 7:18

The book of Micah in the first reading speaks of God's gracious nature in pardoning sin and removing guilt. This passage highlights God's willingness to forgive and His delight in showing mercy to His people.

"The Lord is kind and merciful, slow to anger, and rich in compassion." - Psalm 103:8

The psalmist acknowledges God's kindness, mercy, and compassion. It serves as a reminder that God's nature is one of patience, slow to anger, and rich in love and forgiveness.

"But while he was still a long way off, his father caught sight of him and was filled with compassion. He ran to his son, embraced him, and kissed him." - Luke 15:20

In today's Gospel of Luke, we encounter the parable of the Prodigal Son, which beautifully illustrates God's boundless love and mercy. The father's immediate forgiveness and compassion upon his son's return exemplify God's nature as a loving and forgiving Father.

Prayer:
Heavenly Father, on this Saturday of Lent, we reflect on the themes of your forgiveness and mercy. We are humbled by the boundless love and compassion you extend to your children. Help

us to seek your forgiveness and to extend forgiveness to others in the spirit of reconciliation. May we recognize that you are the God who removes guilt and pardons sin, and that your love and mercy are beyond measure. May our Lenten journey be marked by a deeper appreciation of your forgiveness and a willingness to show mercy to those around us. Through Christ our Lord. Amen.

Action for the Day:
1. Reflect on areas in your life where you may need to seek God's forgiveness and offer your repentance.
2. Consider extending forgiveness and showing mercy to others, especially those you may have conflicts with.
3. Spend time in prayer, expressing gratitude for God's boundless love and mercy.

Sunday, March 3

Third Sunday of Lent

First Reading: Exodus 20:1-17 or 20:1-3, 7-8, 12-17
Responsorial Psalm: Psalm 19:8, 9, 10, 11
Second Reading: 1 Corinthians 1:22-25
Gospel: John 2:13-25

Reflection: Cleansing the Temple
On this Third Sunday of Lent, the Gospel reading leads us to the story of Jesus cleansing the temple. His actions serve as a powerful reminder of the need for spiritual purification and the importance of reverence for God's presence.
"Take these things away; you shall not make my Father's house a

house of trade." - John 2:16

In the Gospel of John, we witness Jesus' righteous anger as He drives out those who have turned the temple into a marketplace. This event highlights the need for holiness and respect in God's house.

"The law of the LORD is perfect, refreshing the soul; the decree of the LORD is trustworthy, giving wisdom to the simple." - Psalm 19:8

The psalmist reflects on the perfection of God's law and the wisdom it imparts to those who embrace it. God's commandments are a source of renewal and spiritual vitality.

"We proclaim Christ crucified, a stumbling block to Jews and foolishness to Gentiles, but to those who are called, Jews and Greeks alike, Christ the power of God and the wisdom of God." - 1 Corinthians 1:23-24

In his letter to the Corinthians in the second reading, Paul acknowledges the paradox of Christ's message. While it may be a stumbling block to some, it is the power and wisdom of God for those who believe.

Prayer:

Heavenly Father, on this Third Sunday of Lent, we reflect on the story of Jesus cleansing the temple. We recognize the need for spiritual purification and reverence for your presence. Help us to embrace your perfect law and find renewal for our souls. May we never turn your house into a marketplace but always seek to honor and worship you in holiness and truth. Grant us the wisdom to see Christ as the power and wisdom of God. Through Christ our Lord. Amen.

Action for the Day:

1. Reflect on the areas in your life that may need spiritual purification and renewal.
2. Consider how you can cultivate a greater reverence for God's presence in your daily life.
3. Pray for vocations to the priesthood, the permanent diaconate, and the consecrated life.

Monday, March 4

Monday of the Third Week of Lent

First Reading: 2 Kings 5:1-15ab

Responsorial Psalm: Psalm 42:2, 3; 43:3, 4

Gospel: Luke 4:24-30

Reflection: Embracing God's Healing Mercy

On this Monday of the third week of Lent, we turn to the story of Naaman, an army commander, who sought healing from the prophet Elisha. This narrative highlights the themes of humility, faith, and unexpected mercy.

"She said to her mistress, 'If only my master would present himself to the prophet in Samaria! He would cure him of his leprosy.'" - 2 Kings 5:3

Naaman's servant speaks with hope about the possibility of his master's healing through the prophet Elisha in Samaria. Despite his prestigious position, Naaman humbles himself and follows the advice of a young Israelite girl. His journey to the prophet Elisha becomes a journey of both physical and spiritual healing.

"I will go to the altar of God, to God, my joy, my delight. Then I will praise you with the harp, O God, my God." - Psalm 43:4

In the psalm, we find a beautiful expression of the psalmist's longing for God's presence. As we journey through Lent, let our hearts echo this desire to draw near to the altar of God, finding joy and delight in His mercy and grace.

"Amen, I say to you, no prophet is accepted in his own native place." - Luke 4:24

In the Gospel of Luke, Jesus encounters resistance in His hometown of Nazareth. The people struggle to accept Him as a prophet, and Jesus challenges their lack of faith. This passage prompts us to examine our own openness to the transformative power of God's word in our lives.

Prayer:

Heavenly Father, on this Monday of the Third Week of Lent, we delve into stories of humility, faith, and unexpected mercy. Like Naaman, may we humbly approach you, seeking healing and redemption. Let our journey through Lent be a pilgrimage to your altar, a place of joy and delight. As we reflect on Jesus' challenges in Nazareth, help us to be open to your transformative word and embrace the merciful love you offer. Through Christ our Lord. Amen.

Action for the Day:

1. Reflect on areas in your life where you may need healing or renewal, whether physically, emotionally, or spiritually.

2. Consider how you can approach God with greater humility and faith, trusting in His power to heal and restore.

3. Spend time in prayer, seeking God's healing touch and expressing your trust in His plan.

First Reading: Daniel 3:25, 34-43
Responsorial Psalm: Psalm 25:4-5ab, 6 and 7bc, 8-9
Gospel: Matthew 18:21-35

Reflection: Forgiveness and Mercy

On this Tuesday of the Third Week of Lent, the Scriptures invite us to reflect on forgiveness, mercy, and the boundless love of God.

"Do not take away your mercy from us, for the sake of Abraham, your beloved, Isaac your servant, and Israel your holy one," -

Daniel 3:35

In the reading from Daniel, we encounter the prayer of Azariah, who, along with his companions, found themselves in the fiery furnace. In their humility and trust, they acknowledge God's abundant mercy, which made the angel of the Lord to go down into the furnace and saved Azariah and his companions. As we face the trials of life, may we too turn to God's mercy for deliverance.

"Make known to me your ways, LORD; teach me your paths. Guide me by your fidelity and teach me, for you are God my savior." - Psalm 25:4-5ab

The psalmist's words express a deep longing for God's guidance and truth. As we navigate the journey of Lent, may we seek God's ways and allow His truth to illuminate our path, leading us to a

45

spirit of forgiveness and reconciliation.

"Then in anger his master handed him over to the torturers until he should pay back the whole debt. So will my heavenly Father do to you, unless each of you forgives his brother from his heart." -

Matthew 18:34-35

In the Gospel of Matthew, Jesus tells a parable emphasizing the importance of forgiveness. The unforgiving servant is a stark reminder of God's mercy towards us and the expectation that we extend that mercy to others. The call to forgive is not just a duty but an expression of the transformed heart.

Prayer:

Heavenly Father, as we reflect on the themes of forgiveness and mercy. We acknowledge our need for your forgiveness and the importance of extending forgiveness to others. May we be inspired by the words of the Lord's Prayer and seek reconciliation with those we may have wronged. Fill us with the vision of your glory and help us to understand the connection between justice and mercy. Grant us the grace to seek your abundant mercy and to become instruments of forgiveness and reconciliation. Through Christ our Lord. Amen.

Action for the Day:

1. Reflect on any unforgiveness or grudges you may be holding and consider how you can extend forgiveness to those who have wronged you.

2. Pray the Lord's Prayer, meditating on the significance of forgiveness within it.

3. Seek ways to show mercy and kindness to others today.

First Reading: Deuteronomy 4:1, 5-9

Responsorial Psalm: Psalm 147:12-13, 15-16, 19-20

Gospel: Matthew 5:17-19

Reflection: God's Commandments and Our Response

On this Wednesday of the third week of Lent, our focus turns to the importance of God's commandments and our response to His guidance.

"Now therefore, Israel, hear the statutes and ordinances I am teaching you to observe, that you may live..." - Deuteronomy 4:1

In the book of Deuteronomy, we are reminded of the importance of God's statutes and decrees, which are given for the well-being and life of His people.

"He proclaims his word to Jacob, his statutes and laws to Israel. He has not done this for any other nation; of such laws they know nothing. Hallelujah!" - Psalm 147:19-20

The psalmist acknowledges God's unique relationship with the people of Israel and the special revelation of His ordinances and statutes. This highlights the special covenant between God and His chosen people.

"Do not think that I have come to abolish the law or the prophets. I have come not to abolish but to fulfill. Amen, I say to you, until heaven and earth pass away, not the smallest letter or the smallest part of a letter will pass from the law, until all things have taken place." - Matthew 5:17-18

47

In the Gospel of Matthew, Jesus affirms the enduring nature of God's commandments and the importance of not neglecting them. He emphasizes that He has come to fulfill the law, not to abolish it.

Prayer:

Heavenly Father, on this Wednesday of Lent, we reflect on the significance of your commandments and our response to your guidance. We acknowledge the life-giving nature of your statutes and decrees. Help us to heed your word and to live in accordance with your commandments. We are grateful for the special covenant you have with your people. May we embrace your teachings, knowing that they remain relevant and enduring. Grant us the grace to honor your law and to follow the example of Jesus, who came to fulfill it. Through Christ our Lord. Amen.

Action for the Day:

1. Are you really living according to the law of Christ? How can you best treasure the law of God in your life? Spend time in reflection on God's commandments and how they guide your life.
2. Consider areas in your life where you can more fully embrace and live out the principles of God's law.
3. Seek to deepen your understanding of the teachings of Jesus and how they relate to God's commandments.

Thursday, March 7

Thursday of the Third Week of Lent

First Reading: Jeremiah 7:23-28

Responsorial Psalm: Psalm 95:1-2, 6-7, 8-9

Gospel: Luke 11:14-23

Reflection: Hear and Follow the Word of God

On this Thursday of the third week of Lent, we are called to reflect on the importance of not only hearing the Word of God but also following it faithfully.

"This is the nation which does not listen to the voice of the LORD, its God, or take correction." - Jeremiah 7:28

The prophet Jeremiah, in the first reading, speaks about a nation that has turned away from the voice of the Lord and does not heed correction. It serves as a reminder of the consequences of not following God's guidance.

"If today you hear his voice, harden not your hearts." - Psalm 95:7-8

The psalmist calls us to remain open to God's voice, emphasizing the need to avoid hardening our hearts when we encounter His message.

"Whoever is not with me is against me, and whoever does not gather with me scatters." - Luke 11:23

In the Gospel of Luke, Jesus speaks about the importance of being aligned with Him. Those who do not gather with Him scatter. It highlights the need for a faithful response to the teachings of Christ.

Prayer:

Heavenly Father, as we reflect on the vital importance of hearing and following your word. We acknowledge the consequences of turning away from your guidance and the need to remain open to your voice. Help us to have hearts that are receptive to your message and willing to follow your path. May we align ourselves with Jesus, gathering with Him in faith and obedience. Grant us the grace to be faithful followers of your word, for it is in hearing and following you that we find true life. Through Christ our Lord. Amen.

Action for the Day:
1. Spend time in prayer, seeking to hear God's voice and open your heart to His message.
2. Reflect on areas in your life where you may need to make changes to align more closely with the teachings of Jesus.
3. Consider how you can actively gather with Christ by participating in acts of love, service, and faith.

Friday, March 8

Friday of the Third Week of Lent

First Reading: Hosea 14:2-10

Responsorial Psalm: Psalm 81:6c-8a, 8bc-9, 10-11ab, 14 and 17

Gospel: Mark 12:28-34

Reflection: The Greatest Commandment – Love God and Neighbor

Today, we turn our attention to the greatest commandment, which calls us to love God and our neighbor with all our hearts.

"I will heal their apostasy, I will love them freely; for my anger is turned away from them." - Hosea 14:5

In the book of Hosea, we encounter God's promise to heal and love His people, even after their apostasy. It highlights God's boundless love and forgiveness.

"I am the Lord, your God: hear my voice." - Psalm 81:11ab

The psalmist's plea to hear God's voice and follow His guidance reflects the importance of aligning our lives with the Lord.

"You are not far from the kingdom of God." - Mark 12:34

In the Gospel of Mark, Jesus acknowledges the wisdom of a scribe who recognizes the significance of loving God and neighbor as the greatest commandment.

Prayer:

Heavenly Father, today, we reflect on the greatest commandment to love you and our neighbors with all our hearts. We are grateful for your promise to heal and love us, even when we have turned away. May we hear your voice and respond with love and obedience. Help us to recognize the wisdom of loving you and our neighbors, as it brings us closer to the kingdom of God. Grant us the grace to live out this commandment in our daily lives, seeking to reflect your boundless love. Through Christ our Lord. Amen.

Action for the Day:

1. Reflect on the ways you can express love for God and your neighbors in your actions and interactions.
2. Consider any areas in your life where you may need to seek healing and reconciliation, both with God and with others.
3. Reach out to a neighbor or friend to show love and care through a kind gesture or act of service.

First Reading: Hosea 6:1-6

Responsorial Psalm: Psalm 51:3-4, 18-19, 20-21ab

Gospel: Luke 18:9-14

Reflection: Repentance and Humility

On this Saturday of the third week of Lent, we reflect on the themes of repentance and humility, guided by today's readings.

"Let us know, let us strive to know the Lord; as certain as the dawn is his coming." - Hosea 6:3

The prophet Hosea calls us to know the Lord and strive for that knowledge. It signifies the importance of seeking a deeper relationship with God.

"My sacrifice, O God, is a contrite spirit; a contrite, humbled heart, O God, you will not scorn." - Psalm 51:19

The psalmist's words express the significance of a contrite and humble heart in God's eyes. It is a heartfelt expression of repentance and humility.

"...the one who humbles himself will be exalted." - Luke 18:14

In the Gospel of Luke, Jesus teaches the importance of humility in prayer. The tax collector who humbly seeks God's mercy is exalted, highlighting the value of a repentant heart.

Prayer:

Heavenly Father, today, we reflect on the themes of repentance and humility. We recognize the importance of seeking to know you and striving for a deeper relationship. Grant us the grace to come before you with contrite and humble hearts, knowing that you will not scorn such offerings. Help us to follow the example of the tax collector in Luke's Gospel, who sought your mercy with humility. May we embrace the path of repentance and find the exaltation that comes from humbly turning to you. Through Christ our Lord. Amen.

Action for the Day:
1. Reflect on areas in your life where you may need to seek God's forgiveness and offer your repentance.
2. Spend time in prayer, expressing your contrition and humility before God.
3. When was the last time you sought God's mercy in the Sacrament of Reconciliation? Schedule a time to go to confession.

Sunday, March 10

Fourth Sunday of Lent (Laetare Sunday)

First Reading: 2 Chronicles 36:14-16, 19-23
Responsorial Psalm: Psalm 137:1-2, 3, 4-5, 6
Second Reading: Ephesians 2:4-10
Gospel: John 3:14-21

Reflection: Rejoicing in God's Mercy and Love
The Fourth Sunday of Lent (also known as Laetare Sunday) is the midpoint of the Lenten season. It's a time to reflect on God's boundless mercy and love, even as you continue your Lenten spiritual journey.

"Early and often the Lord, the God of their ancestors, sent his messengers to them, for he had compassion on his people and his dwelling place." - 2 Chronicles 36:15

The first reading taken from 2 Chronicles reminds us of God's persistence in reaching out to His people with compassion and love, even when they have strayed.

"For by grace you have been saved through faith, and this is not from you; it is the gift of God." - Ephesians 2:8

The second reading of the day taken from Paul's letter to the Ephesians emphasizes that our salvation is a gift of God's grace, and it comes through faith. It's a reminder of the unmerited nature of God's love.

"For God so loved the world that he gave his only Son so that everyone who believes in him might not perish but might have eternal life." - John 3:16

In the Gospel of John, we encounter one of the most beloved and profound verses in the Bible, which encapsulates the essence of God's love and His gift of salvation through His Son.

Prayer:

Heavenly Father, on this Laetare Sunday, the Fourth Sunday of Lent, we rejoice in your boundless mercy and love. We are grateful for the gift of your Son, Jesus Christ, through whom we find eternal life. May we never forget the depth of your love, which sent messengers and persistently reached out to us with compassion. Help us to embrace your grace, which is the source of our salvation. Grant us the grace to believe in you and experience the joy of knowing that we are saved through faith. Through Christ our Lord. Amen.

Action for the Day:

1. Take a moment to reflect on God's love and mercy in your life and express your gratitude.
2. Do an honest check-in with yourself today on your Lenten spiritual journey so far.
3. As Lent reaches its halfway point, recommit yourself to prayer, fasting, and almsgiving to purify your heart for the Paschal feast.

Monday, March 11

Monday of the Fourth Week of Lent

First Reading: Isaiah 65:17-21
Responsorial Psalm: Psalm 30:2 and 4, 5-6, 11-12a and 13b
Gospel: John 4:43-54

Reflection: Faith and Healing

On this Monday of the Fourth Week of Lent, the Scriptures invite us to contemplate the transformative power of faith, healing, and the steadfast love of God.

"See, I am creating new heavens and a new earth; the former things shall not be remembered nor come to mind." - Isaiah 65:17
In the words of the prophet Isaiah, we glimpse a vision of God's redemptive work, creating a new heavens and a new earth. This prophecy echoes the promise of renewal and restoration that comes through the grace of God.

"I praise you, Lord, for you raised me up and did not let my

enemies rejoice over me." - Psalm 30:2

The psalmist's expression of gratitude reflects the joy and deliverance that come from the Lord. In times of trouble, God's intervention not only brings healing but also prevents the triumph of our enemies. This acknowledgment inspires a song of praise.

"Jesus said to him, 'You may go; your son will live.' The man believed what Jesus said to him and left." - John 4:50

In the Gospel of John, we encounter a royal official who seeks Jesus' help for the healing of his son. Jesus, demonstrating the power of faith, assures the man that his son will live. The man believed Jesus' words, and upon returning home, discovered the fulfillment of the promise.

Prayer:

Heavenly Father, today, we reflect on the power of faith and the assurance of your healing touch. We are grateful for your enduring love and mercy that lasts a lifetime. Help us to place our faith in you, just as the royal official did when he sought Jesus for the healing of his son. We recognize that your knowledge and purpose for our lives extend from the very beginning. Grant us the grace to trust in your plan and to believe in the power of your word. Through Christ our Lord. Amen.

Action for the Day:

1. Reflect on the role of faith in your life and consider areas where you can deepen your trust in God's plan.
2. Reach out to someone in need, offering them support and encouragement.
3. Spend time in prayer, seeking God's healing touch for any

concerns or difficulties you may be facing.

First Reading: Ezekiel 47:1-9, 12
Responsorial Psalm: Psalm 46:2-3, 5-6, 8-9
Gospel: John 5:1-16

Reflection: Healing at the Pool of Bethesda
On this Tuesday of the fourth week of Lent, we delve into the story of a man who experienced healing at the Pool of Bethesda, highlighting the theme of God's restorative power.

"One man was there who had been ill for thirty-eight years." -
John 5:5

The Gospel of John introduces us to a man who had been suffering from illness for nearly four decades, illustrating the depth of his need for healing.

"Sir, I have no one to put me into the pool when the water is stirred up; while I am on my way, someone else gets down there before me."- John 5:7

The man at the pool explains his situation, expressing his hope for healing. Although he wants to be healed, he knew that there would be many who will try to be the first when an angel stirs the water is up.

"Rise, take up your mat, and walk." - John 5:8

These are the words Jesus spoke to the man, immediately granting him the ability to walk and be healed. Today, Jesus is asking if you are ready to be healed and He is waiting for your answer.

Unfortunately, most times we give God excuses just like the man in the story who said that he has no one to put him into the pool when the water is stirred up. But God can always surprise us. There is no end to his creative ability.

Prayer:

Heavenly Father, today, we reflect on the story of the man at the Pool of Bethesda, who experienced the miraculous healing power of Jesus. We acknowledge that there are times in our lives when we, too, need your healing touch. Grant us the strength to reach out to you in faith, just as the man by the pool did. May we be open to your word and ready to receive the healing you offer. Help us to trust in your restorative power and to follow your guidance in our lives. Through Christ our Lord. Amen.

Action for the Day:
1. Reflect on areas in your life where you may need healing, whether physical, emotional, or spiritual, and offer them to God in prayer.
2. Schedule a time to go to confession and discover Jesus' healing in the Sacrament of Penance. Confession is the answer to the freedom that awaits you, especially when it is entered into honestly and thoroughly.
3. Spend time in prayer, seeking God's guidance and healing for yourself and others.

Wednesday, March 13

Wednesday of the Fourth Week of Lent

First Reading: Isaiah 49:8-15

Responsorial Psalm: Psalm 145:8-9, 13cd-14, 17-18

Gospel: John 5:17-30

Reflection: The Compassion of God

On this Wednesday of the fourth week of Lent, we envision the boundless compassion of God as revealed in the Scriptures.

"Can a mother forget her infant, be without tenderness for the child of her womb? Even should she forget, I will never forget you." - Isaiah 49:15

The first reading taken from the book of Isaiah speaks of God's unwavering love and compassion, even comparing it to a mother's love for her child.

"The Lord is gracious and merciful, slow to anger and abounding in mercy. The Lord is good to all, compassionate toward all your works." - Psalm 145:8-9

The psalmist extols the compassion and kindness of the Lord, recognizing His goodness to all and His care for His creation.

"Amen, amen, I say to you, whoever hears my word and believes in the one who sent me has eternal life and will not come to condemnation, but has passed from death to life." - John 5:24

In the reading from the Gospel of John, Jesus assures us of the eternal life granted to those who hear His word and believe in the One who sent Him. It's a testament to God's compassion and the gift of salvation.

Prayer:

Heavenly Father, today, we meditate on your boundless compassion as revealed in your word. We are grateful for the image of a mother's love, which reflects your deep care for us. Your graciousness, mercy, and kindness inspire us to draw closer to you. We believe in your Son, Jesus Christ, who offers us eternal life and salvation. Help us to embrace your compassion and share it with others in our daily lives. May we be living witnesses to your goodness. Through Christ our Lord. Amen.

Action for the Day:
1. Reflect on God's compassion and how it has been evident in your life.
2. Consider how you can extend compassion and kindness to those in need, following God's example.
3. Spend time in prayer, thanking God for His compassion and seeking His guidance in living a more compassionate life.

Thursday, March 14

Thursday of the Fourth Week of Lent

First Reading: Exodus 32:7-14

Responsorial Psalm: Psalm 106:19-20, 21-22, 23

Gospel: John 5:31-47

Reflection: God's Mercy and the Path to Belief

Today, we reflect on God's mercy and the journey of belief as portrayed in the Scriptures.

"...I will make of you a great nation." - Exodus 32:10

In the first reading taken from the book of Exodus, we witness God's mercy as He offers Moses the opportunity to intercede for the people of Israel, despite their unfaithfulness.

"I do not accept testimony from a human being, but I say this so that you may be saved." - John 5:34

In the Gospel of John, Jesus speaks about the purpose of His testimony and teaching, which is ultimately for the salvation of humanity.

Prayer:

Heavenly Father, today, we reflect on your enduring mercy and the path to belief. We are reminded not to forget the works of the Lord and to acknowledge your unwavering love. Just as you offered mercy to the people of Israel through Moses, we know that your mercy extends to us as well. May we heed the testimony of Jesus, which is given for our salvation. Help us to believe in Him and to walk the path of faith, trusting in your mercy. Through Christ our Lord. Amen.

Action for the Day:

1. Reflect on instances in your life where you have experienced God's mercy and wondrous works.

2. Spend time in prayer, reflect on your life and ask yourself the following questions:

   i.   Do you live your life to gain the outward praise of others or the quiet praise of God?

   ii. Do you allow your pride get in the way and to do things to please others which may not please God?

   iii. Do you gossip or criticize good people to win the friendship of someone?

   iv. Do you feel pressured to do things you don't

necessarily feel comfortable doing, giving into peer pressure when you know it is wrong?

3. Examine your life today and pray for the grace to keep growing in the freedom to be your own person, to speak your truth and witness to the risen Jesus.

First Reading: Wisdom 2:1a, 12-22

Responsorial Psalm: Psalm 34:17-18, 19-20, 21 and 23

Gospel: John 7:1-2, 10, 25-30

Reflection: Facing Opposition with Faith

Today, we reflect on the theme of facing opposition with faith, as portrayed in the readings of today.

"With violence and torture let us put him to the test that we may have proof of his gentleness and try his patience." - Wisdom 2:19

The Book of Wisdom describes the unjust treatment of the just one, highlighting the test of gentleness and patience that he endures.

"The righteous cry out, the Lord hears and he rescues them from all their afflictions." - Psalm 34:18

The psalmist reminds us of God's proximity to the righteous and His role as a Savior for those who are afflicted.

"I know him, because I am from him, and he sent me." - John 7:29

In the Gospel of John, Jesus asserts His knowledge of God the Father, emphasizing His divine origin and mission.

The gospel further speaks about the wickedness of the Jews and their plot to kill Jesus, the just one, because he seems different from all of them. The Jews did not understand Jesus. They just want to blot Him out of the world. Sometimes we are like the Jews during the time of Jesus. We become indifferent to his love and friendship. He wants to be close with us but we want to turn away. Jesus showed in His lifetime what it really means to be a true friend. He is always in our midst to embrace us though we are all sinners. In this time of lent, we are all invited to change our hearts and believe in the one who first loved us.

Prayer:

Heavenly Father, today, we reflect on the challenge of facing opposition with faith. We are mindful of the unjust treatment the just one endured and the test of gentleness and patience. Help us to remember that you are close to the righteous and a Savior to those who are afflictions. We are grateful for Jesus, who came from you and was sent on a divine mission. May we trust in His knowledge and mission, finding strength and faith in the face of opposition. Through Christ our Lord. Amen.

Action for the Day:

1. Reflect on moments when you have faced opposition in your faith journey and how you responded.
2. Consider how you can support and encourage others who may be enduring challenges to their faith.
3. Spend time in prayer, reflect on your life and ask yourself the following questions:
    i. Are you afraid of speaking the truth for fear of what others will say or think about you?

ii. Is there an opportunity for you to lovingly reach out and bring the truth of Christ's message to someone you know?

First Reading: Jeremiah 11:18-20
Responsorial Psalm: Psalm 7:2-3, 9bc-10, 11-12
Gospel: John 7:40-53

Reflection: Seeking the Truth and Justice
On this Saturday of the fourth week of Lent, we explore the theme of seeking the truth and justice, as exemplified in the Scriptures.
"But, you, LORD of hosts, just Judge, searcher of mind and heart, let me witness the vengeance you take on them, for to you I have entrusted my cause!" - Jeremiah 11:20
The prophet Jeremiah expresses his trust in God, who is a just Judge and searcher of heart, seeking vengeance on behalf of the righteous.
"Let the malice of the wicked end. Uphold the just one, O just God, who tries hearts and minds." - Psalm 7:10
The psalmist acknowledges that God will one day end all evil, and those who honor God will be secure forever. This verse also that the righteous God tries hearts and minds. He knows what every person is thinking, and He discerns the thoughts and motives of every person's heart.
"Never before has anyone spoken like this one." - John 7:46
In the Gospel of John, the officers sent to arrest Jesus were struck

by His words and acknowledge that no one has ever spoken like Him. The officers approached Jesus at the very time when He was addressing the people. They were so impressed and awed with what He said that they dared not arrest Him. His speaking had so much evidence of truth, so much proof that he was from God, and was so impressive and persuasive, that they were convinced of his innocence.

Prayer:

Heavenly Father, today, we reflect on the quest for truth and justice. We place our trust in you, the one who tries the just and seeks vengeance on their behalf. You are a God who judges justly and shields those with upright hearts. We are inspired by the words of Jesus, which are unlike any others. May we seek the truth and wisdom that comes from you. Grant us the grace to trust in your righteous judgment and to stand up for truth in our lives. Through Christ our Lord. Amen.

Action for the Day:

1. Reflect on moments in your life when you have sought the truth and pursued justice.
2. Consider how you can be a source of truth and justice in your interactions and decisions.
3. Spend time in prayer, seeking God's guidance in your quest for truth and justice, both for yourself and for others.

Sunday, March 17

Fifth Sunday of Lent

First Reading: Jeremiah 31:31-34

Responsorial Psalm: Psalm 51:3-4, 12-13, 14-15

Second Reading: Hebrews 5:7-9

Gospel: John 12:20-33

Reflection: The New Covenant and the Way of the Cross

On this Fifth Sunday of Lent, the Scriptures draw us into a profound reflection on the new covenant, repentance, and the sacrificial love of Christ.

"See, days are coming—oracle of the Lord—when I will make a new covenant with the house of Israel and the house of Judah." - Jeremiah 31:31

In the prophecy of Jeremiah, we glimpse the promise of a new covenant. God foretells a time when His law will be written on the hearts of His people, emphasizing a transformative relationship founded on intimacy and genuine knowledge of God.

"Create in me a clean heart, O God, and renew a steadfast spirit within me." - Psalm 51:12

The psalmist, pours out his heart in repentance, acknowledging the need for a clean heart and a steadfast spirit. In this plea, we find the essence of Lent—a season of introspection, repentance, and the desire for God's renewing grace.

"In the days when he was in the flesh, he offered prayers and supplications with loud cries and tears to the one who was able to save him from death, and he was heard because of his reverence." - Hebrews 5:7

In the Paul's letter to the Hebrews in the second reading, the profound humanity of Jesus is revealed. The passage describes Christ's prayers and supplications with deep reverence, highlighting the intensity of His connection with the Father.

"Unless a grain of wheat falls to the ground and dies, it remains just a grain of wheat; but if it dies, it produces much fruit." - John 12:24

In the Gospel of John, Jesus uses the metaphor of a grain of wheat to illustrate the transformative power of sacrifice. His impending death on the cross is the path to new life—a life that bears much fruit.

Prayer:

Gracious God, on this Fifth Sunday of Lent, we contemplate the beauty of the new covenant, the depth of repentance, and the sacrificial love of Christ. As we journey through this season, write your law on our hearts, creating in us clean hearts and steadfast spirits. Like Jesus in His humanity, may our prayers and supplications be marked by reverence and trust in your saving power. Help us to understand the profound truth that through the way of the cross, new life and abundant fruit are brought forth. Through Christ our Lord. Amen.

Action for the Day:

1. Reflect on the state of your heart and spirit. In what ways do you seek renewal during this Lenten season?
2. Spend time in prayer, offering your repentance and seeking God's transforming grace.
3. Contemplate the metaphor of the grain of wheat. How can you embrace the way of the cross in your life to bear fruit for God's kingdom?

First Reading: Daniel 13:1-9, 15-17, 19-30, 33-62 or 13:41c-62

Responsorial Psalm: Psalm 23:1-3a, 3b-4, 5, 6

Gospel: John 8:1-11

Reflection: Encounter with Mercy and Truth

On this Monday of the Fifth Week of Lent, the Scriptures invite us to contemplate the themes of justice, mercy, and the transformative power of encounter with the truth.

"The Lord is my shepherd; I shall not want." - *Psalm 23:1*

The familiar words of Psalm 23 begin our reflection, reminding us of the shepherd's care for his sheep, ensuring that we lack nothing under His watchful care. As we enter into the narratives of Daniel and John, we are encouraged to trust in the guiding and protective hand of the Good Shepherd.

"But Susanna cried aloud: "Eternal God, you know what is hidden and are aware of all things before they come to be: you know that they have testified falsely against me. Here I am about to die, though I have done none of the things for which these men have condemned me." - *Daniel 13:42-43*

The first reading narrates the story of Susanna, where we witness a tale of righteousness and the pursuit of justice. Susanna, falsely accused, remains steadfast in her integrity. The narrative unfolds, revealing the profound importance of truth and the eventual triumph of justice through the wisdom of Daniel.

"Let the one among you who is without sin be the first to throw a

stone at her." - John 8:7

In John's Gospel, we encounter the woman caught in adultery. The religious leaders bring her before Jesus, testing Him. In response, Jesus invites the one without sin to cast the first stone, leading to a transformative moment of mercy and forgiveness.

Prayer:

Gracious Lord, today, we approach you with hearts open to the lessons of justice and mercy. As the shepherd cares for the sheep, may we trust in your guidance and protection. In the stories of Susanna and the woman caught in adultery, we see the tension between justice and mercy. Teach us to navigate these complexities with integrity and compassion. Grant us the courage to stand for truth and the humility to extend mercy, recognizing that we too are recipients of your unmerited grace. Through Christ our Lord. Amen.

Action for the Day:

1. Reflect on situations in your life where justice and mercy intersect. How can you respond with integrity and compassion?

2. Consider moments when you may have judged others. Pray for the grace to embrace a spirit of mercy and understanding.

3. Reach out to someone in need of compassion, offering a listening ear and support.

Tuesday, March 19

Solemnity of Saint Joseph, husband of the Blessed Virgin
Mary

First Reading: 2 Samuel 7:4-5a, 12-14a, 16

Responsorial Psalm: Psalm 89:2-3, 4-5, 27 and 29

Second Reading: Romans 4:13, 16-18, 22

Gospel: Matthew 1:16, 18-21, 24a or Luke 2:41-51a

Reflection: The Faith of Saint Joseph and God's Promise

On this Tuesday of the Fifth Week of Lent and the Solemnity of
Saint Joseph, husband of the Blessed Virgin Mary, the Scriptures
illuminate the faithfulness of Saint Joseph and the fulfillment of
God's promises.

"I will be a father to him, and he shall be a son to me." - 2 Samuel
7:14a

In the passage from 2 Samuel, we encounter the promise of God to
David, foretelling the establishment of a kingdom and a dynasty.
This promise ultimately finds its fulfillment in Jesus, the Son of
God, whose earthly father, Joseph, plays a significant role in God's
plan.

"I will make your dynasty stand forever and establish your
throne through all ages." - Psalm 89:5

The psalm echoes the everlasting nature of God's promise,
emphasizing the eternal significance of David's throne. In Joseph's
acceptance of his role as the foster father of Jesus, we witness the
unfolding of God's plan for salvation.

"It was not through the law that the promise was made to
Abraham and his descendants that he would inherit the world,

but through the righteousness that comes from faith." - Romans 4:13

In the Paul's letter to the Romans in the second reading, the concept of faith as justification is explored. This theological reflection speaks to the profound faith of Saint Joseph, who, without fully understanding, obediently embraced his role in God's salvific plan.

"Joseph, son of David, do not be afraid to take Mary your wife into your home." - Matthew 1:20b

In the Gospel of Matthew, we explore the moment when Joseph learns of Mary's pregnancy. Despite the confusion and potential scandal, Joseph's obedience to the angel's message is an extraordinary testament to his trust in God's divine plan.

Prayer:

Heavenly Father, on this Solemnity of Saint Joseph, we celebrate the faithfulness of this righteous man who played a pivotal role in your plan for salvation. Just as you made a covenant with David, You established Joseph as the earthly father of Jesus, fulfilling the promise of a Savior. Help us, like Saint Joseph, to trust in your promises even when we do not fully comprehend your plan. May we embrace our roles in your unfolding story of redemption with unwavering faith and obedience. Through Christ our Lord. Amen.

Action for the Day:

1. Reflect on the role of faith in your life. In what areas do you need to trust more in God's promises?

2. Consider Saint Joseph's obedience to God's plan. How can you emulate his trust and obedience in your own journey of

faith?

3. Pray for guidance and strength to follow God's will with the same faith and obedience as Saint Joseph.

First Reading: Daniel 3:14-20, 91-92, 95
Responsorial Psalm: Daniel 3:52, 53, 54, 55, 56
Gospel: John 8:31-42

Reflection: True Freedom in the Truth

On this Wednesday of the Fifth Week of Lent, the Scriptures invite us to reflect on the theme of true freedom found in the truth of God's Word.

"Blessed be the God of Shadrach, Meshach, and Abednego, who sent his angel to deliver the servants that trusted in him." - Daniel
3:95

The passage from Daniel recounts the courageous stand of Shadrach, Meshach, and Abednego, who, facing the threat of death, choose to remain faithful to God. The fiery furnace becomes a symbol of their unwavering commitment and the divine protection that accompanies their fidelity.

The responsorial psalm of today is also known as the Canticle of Azariah, found in Daniel, is a hymn of praise and thanksgiving for God's deliverance. It echoes the sentiments of gratitude and acknowledgment of God's sovereignty even in the midst of adversity.

"If you remain in my word, you will truly be my disciples, and

you will know the truth, and the truth will set you free." - John 8:31-32

In the Gospel of John, Jesus speaks about the transformative power of truth and the freedom that comes from being disciples who abide in His Word. This freedom is not merely a worldly concept but a profound liberation found in the truth of God's eternal promises.

Prayer:

Gracious God, on this Wednesday of the Fifth Week of Lent, we come before you with hearts open to the truth that brings true freedom. As Jesus taught His disciples, may we abide in your Word, knowing that it is the source of genuine liberation. Like Shadrach, Meshach, and Abednego, grant us the courage to stand firm in our faith, trusting in your protection and deliverance. We echo the Canticle of Azariah, praising you for your mercy and steadfast love. Through Christ our Lord. Amen.

Action for the Day:

1. Reflect on areas in your life where you may not be fully abiding in God's Word. How can you deepen your connection to the truth of Scripture?

2. Consider situations where standing for the truth may require courage. Pray for the strength to remain faithful, even in challenging circumstances.

3. Spend time in gratitude, praising God for His mercy and deliverance in your life.

First Reading: Genesis 17:3-9

Responsorial Psalm: Psalm 105:4-5, 6-7, 8-9

Gospel: John 8:51-59

Reflection: Unbreakable Everlasting Covenant

On this Thursday of the Fifth Week of Lent, the Scriptures guide us to reflect on the everlasting covenant God establishes with His people, the importance of remembrance, and the promise of eternal life found in Christ.

"For my part, here is my covenant with you: you are to become the father of a multitude of nations." - Genesis 17:4

In the first reading taken from Genesis, God establishes an unbreakable everlasting covenant with Abraham, promising him, descendants as numerous as the stars. This covenant is a testament to God's faithfulness and the unfolding of His redemptive plan through the generations.

"Seek out the Lord and his might; constantly seek his face." - Psalm 105:4

The psalmist encourages us to seek the Lord continually, acknowledging His strength and sovereignty. This call to constant service is rooted in the remembrance of God's covenant and faithfulness throughout history.

"Amen, amen, I say to you, whoever keeps my word will never see death." - John 8:51

In the Gospel of John, Jesus declares a profound truth about eternal life. He connects the idea of eternal life with keeping His word. The promise of life beyond death is intricately tied to faithfulness and obedience to the teachings of Christ.

Prayer:

Gracious God, on this Thursday of the Fifth Week of Lent, we contemplate the beauty of covenant, the call to constant service, and the promise of eternal life in Christ. Just as you established a covenant with Abraham, may we recognize your faithfulness in our lives. Help us to seek you continually, remembering your strength and sovereignty. As we reflect on the words of Jesus, may we keep your word faithfully, trusting in the promise of eternal life. Through Christ our Lord. Amen.

Action for the Day:

1. Reflect on the covenants God has established with His people throughout Scripture. How do these covenants shape your understanding of God's faithfulness?
2. Consider ways in which you can seek the Lord continually in your daily life. How can you serve Him more faithfully?
3. Meditate on the promise of eternal life in Christ. How does this promise influence your perspective on life and death?

Friday, March 22

Friday of the Fifth Week of Lent

First Reading: Jeremiah 20:10-13
Responsorial Psalm: Psalm 18:2-3a, 3bc-4, 5-6, 7
Gospel: John 10:31-42

Reflection: Faith amidst Opposition

On this Friday of the Fifth Week of Lent, the Scriptures draw our attention to the challenges faced by those who remain faithful to God amidst opposition, and the strength found in trusting the Lord.

"But the LORD is with me, like a mighty champion..." - Jeremiah 20:11

In the first reading from Jeremiah, we glimpse into the prophet's struggle as he faces opposition for delivering God's message. Despite the challenges, Jeremiah finds solace in the presence of the Lord, who is described as a mighty champion, offering protection and support.

"I love you, LORD, my strength." - Psalm 18:2

The psalmist echoes the sentiments of trust and love for the Lord. In times of trouble, the psalmist turns to God as a source of strength and refuge. This declaration of love reflects a deep and personal relationship with the Almighty.

"If I do not perform my Father's works, do not believe me; but if I perform them, even if you do not believe me, believe the works, so that you may realize [and understand] that the Father is in me and I am in the Father." - John 10:37-38

In the Gospel of John, Jesus confronts opposition and seeks to affirm His unity with the Father through His works. Despite the disbelief of some, Jesus emphasizes the tangible evidence of His divine mission in the miracles and signs He performs.

Prayer:

Heavenly Father, on this Friday of the Fifth Week of Lent, we are reminded of the challenges faced by those who stand firm in their faith. Like Jeremiah, may we find comfort in your presence, knowing that you are a mighty champion who stands with us in times of opposition. We declare our love for you, trusting in your strength. In the example of Jesus, may we recognize the evidence of your divine works and be strengthened in our belief. In Jesus' name, we pray. Amen.

Action for the Day:
1. Reflect on a time when your faith was tested or when you faced opposition for your beliefs. How did you find strength in the Lord?
2. Consider the works of Jesus and their impact on your faith. How do His miracles and teachings affirm the truth of His divine mission?
3. Pray for the strength to stand firm in your faith, trusting that the Lord is with you as a mighty champion.

Saturday, March 23

Saturday of the Fifth Week of Lent

First Reading: Ezekiel 37:21-28
Responsorial Psalm: Jeremiah 31:10, 11-12abcd, 13
Gospel: John 11:45-56

Reflection: The Promise of Unity and the Coming of the Lord

On this Saturday of the Fifth Week of Lent, the Scriptures guide us to reflect on the promise of unity among God's people and the approaching fulfillment of God's plan in the coming of the Lord.

"I will make them one nation in the land..." - Ezekiel 37:22

In the first reading from Ezekiel, God promises to reunite the divided tribes of Israel, making them one nation. This prophecy speaks to the restoration and unity that God brings to His people, symbolizing the broader theme of reconciliation through the Lord.

"Hear the word of the LORD, you nations, proclaim it on distant coasts, and say: The One who scattered Israel, now gathers them; he guards them as a shepherd his flock." - Jeremiah 31:10

Jeremiah's words in the responsorial psalm, convey the imagery of God as a caring shepherd who watches over His flock. This comforting image reminds us of God's protective and guiding presence, leading His people with love and compassion.

"So from that day on they planned to kill him." - John 11:53

In the Gospel of John, the opposition to Jesus intensifies as the religious leaders conspire to kill Him. This plot, however, plays a crucial role in God's plan for salvation, leading to the ultimate sacrifice for the unity and redemption of humanity.

Prayer:

Heavenly Father, on this Saturday of the Fifth Week of Lent, we anticipate your promise to make your people one nation. Like the caring shepherd, may you guard and guide us with love and compassion. As we approach the events leading to the cross, help us understand the profound significance of Jesus' sacrifice for our unity and redemption. Open our hearts to receive the fulfillment of your plan in the coming of the Lord. Through Christ our Lord. Amen.

Action for the Day:

1. Reflect on moments of unity and restoration in your life. How has God brought reconciliation in situations of division or brokenness?

2. Consider the image of God as a shepherd guarding His flock. How does this imagery bring comfort and assurance in your journey of faith?

3. Pray for a deeper understanding of the significance of Jesus' sacrifice for unity and redemption. Ask for the grace to embrace the Lord's coming in your life.

4. On this Lenten Friday, fast from social media, television, gaming, or other entertainment and go to confession. This will help you to renew your heart through the sacrament of reconciliation, so as to live fully the abundant grace of the paschal mystery.

Sunday, March 24

Palm Sunday of the Lord's Passion

At the Procession with Palms

Gospel: Mark 11:1-10 or John 12:12-16

At the Mass

First Reading: Isaiah 50:4-7

Responsorial Psalm: Psalm 22:8-9, 17-18, 19-20, 23-24.

Second Reading: Philippians 2:6-11

Gospel: Mark 14:1-15:47 or 15:1-39

Reflection: The Triumphal Entry and the Journey to the Cross

Palm Sunday marks the beginning of Holy Week. Today, we

celebrate Jesus' triumphant entry into Jerusalem. The crowds hailed Him with palm branches and shouts of "Hosanna," recognizing Him as the King who comes in the name of the Lord. Yet, as we move through the liturgy, we shift from celebration to the solemn meditation of Jesus' passion and the events that led to His crucifixion. This is a time to welcome Jesus into our lives and ask Him to allow us a share in his suffering, death and Resurrection. The Holy Week liturgies present us with the actual events of the dying and rising of Jesus. These liturgies enable us to experience in our lives here and now what Jesus went through then. In other words, what we commemorate and relive during this week is not just Jesus' dying and rising, but our own dying and rising in Him, which result in our healing, reconciliation, and redemption. Just as Jesus did, we, too, must lay down our lives freely by actively participating in the Holy Week liturgies. In doing so, we are allowing Jesus to forgive us our sins, heal the wounds in us caused by our sins and transform us more completely into the image and likeness of God. In this way, we will be able to live more fully the divine life we received at Baptism.

"Hosanna! Blessed is he who comes in the name of the Lord!
Blessed is the kingdom of our father David that is to come!
Hosanna in the highest!" - Mark 11: 9b-10

As Jesus entered Jerusalem, the people welcomed Him with shouts of "Hosanna," signifying their recognition of His kingship and their hope for the coming kingdom.

"This is the day the Lord has made; let us rejoice in it and be
glad" - Psalm 118:24

The psalmist's words remind us that Palm Sunday is a day of rejoicing, even as we anticipate the challenges and trials that lie ahead.

"For he knew who would betray him; for this reason, he said,
'Not all of you are clean.'" - John 13:11

The events of the Last Supper, including the washing of the disciples' feet, foreshadow the ultimate sacrifice Jesus will make for our redemption.

Prayer:

Heavenly Father, on this Palm Sunday of the Passion of the Lord, we remember Jesus' triumphant entry into Jerusalem and the acclamations of the crowd. As we begin Holy Week, we are mindful of the challenges and trials that await. May we, too, welcome Jesus as our King, recognizing His divine authority. Grant us the grace to be glad and rejoice in this day, which the Lord has made. Help us to journey with Jesus through the coming days, knowing that His ultimate sacrifice is for our salvation. Through Christ our Lord. Amen.

Action for the Day:

1. Reflect on the significance of Palm Sunday and what it means to welcome Jesus as your King.
2. Attend a Palm Sunday mass or procession if possible, and participate in the blessing of palms.
3. In one week, we will celebrate Easter Sunday. Pray that the Lord allow you to accompany him serenely during these Easter mysteries and you may emerge from them renewed in faith, hope and charity.

First Reading: Isaiah 42:1-7

Responsorial Psalm: Psalm 27:1, 2, 3, 13-14

Gospel: John 12:1-11

Reflection: Anointing and Preparation

Holy Week is here again, and regardless of your commitment to the Lenten practices you made around Ash Wednesday, there is still time to re-center yourself upon the spiritual meaning of Lent. The readings of today invites us into a poignant moment of preparation and anointing in Bethany. It also reflects on the themes of prophetic mission of the servant found in the Scriptures. It reminds us that Jesus has been chosen by the Father as a servant to suffer, and so save the people of God. As the servant's mission unfolds, may our hearts be open to the profound love that leads to the cross.

"Here is my servant whom I uphold, my chosen one with whom I am pleased. Upon him I have put my spirit; he shall bring forth justice to the nations." - Isaiah 42:1

Isaiah's prophecy, in the first reading, paints a vivid picture of the Servant of the Lord, who is anointed by the Spirit to bring forth justice to the nations. This prophecy foreshadows Jesus as the ultimate Servant of God, who came to bring salvation and righteousness to the world.

"The LORD is my light and my salvation; whom should I fear? The LORD is my life's refuge; of whom should I be afraid?" - Psalm 27:1

The psalmist records that our Lord, who is the light of the world, places his trust in God, who is light and salvation for all. The Father will bring the Lord Jesus through suffering into glory. In the face of challenges, the psalm becomes a declaration of faith, seeking the Lord's guidance and finding refuge in His sanctuary. This sentiment resonates with the themes of Holy Week as we embark on the journey toward the cross.

"Mary took a liter of costly perfumed oil made from genuine aromatic nard and anointed the feet of Jesus and dried them with her hair; the house was filled with the fragrance of the oil." - John 12:3

In the Gospel of John, we witness an act of extraordinary devotion and love as Mary anoints Jesus' feet with costly perfumed oil. Judas ridiculed Mary and said that it should have been sold and the money be given to the poor. However, Jesus responds in Mary's defense and commends Mary for her act of love and foresight. This anointing becomes symbolic of Jesus' preparation for His burial.

Prayer:

Heavenly Father, on this Monday of Holy Week, we enter into a time of preparation and reflection. As we envision the mission of the Servant, grant us the grace to trust in your providence, finding refuge in your sanctuary. Like Mary, may we offer our most precious gifts in love and anticipation of the sacrifice that leads to redemption. Through Christ our Lord. Amen.

Action for the Day:

1. Reflect on the ways you can serve others with love and

devotion, following the example of Mary's anointing of Jesus.

2. Take time for silent reflection, meditating on the qualities of the Servant of the Lord described in the book of Isaiah.

3. Spend time in prayer, seeking God's guidance in your life and reflect on how you can offer your most precious gifts to Jesus in your daily life.

Tuesday, March 26

Tuesday of Holy Week

First Reading: Isaiah 49:1-6

Responsorial Psalm: Psalm 71:1-2, 3-4a, 5ab-6ab, 15 and 17

Gospel: John 13:21-33, 36-38

Reflection: The Servant's Mission and Jesus' Imminent Betrayal

On this Tuesday of Holy Week, we are called to reflect on the prophetic mission of the suffering servant and the imminent betrayal of Jesus by one of His own. Like the servant, Jesus embraces His mission with humility and obedience. As we enter deeper into the mysteries of Holy Week, may we, too, surrender ourselves to God's redemptive plan.

"For now the LORD has spoken who formed me as his servant from the womb, That Jacob may be brought back to him and Israel gathered to him; I am honored in the sight of the LORD, and my God is now my strength!" - Isaiah 49:5

Isaiah's prophecy in the first reading, unveils the divine calling of the servant of the Lord. Today's reading not only speaks of the servant's mission to bring Israel back to God but also hints at a universal mission, extending salvation to the ends of the earth. Here, we are meant t understand that Jesus was called from the beginning of his life on earth to bring God's glory to us, and to gather God's people together. As we journey through Holy Week, we recognize Jesus as the ultimate fulfillment of this prophecy.

"My God, rescue me from the hand of the wicked, from the clutches of the evil and violent." - Psalm 71:4

The psalmist's plea for deliverance echoes the human longing for God's intervention. Today's responsorial psalm becomes a prayer of trust, seeking refuge in God's justice and salvation.

"When he had said this, Jesus was deeply troubled and testified, 'Amen, amen, I say to you, one of you will betray me.'" - John 13:21

In the Gospel of John, we witness the solemn moment when Jesus reveals that one of His disciples will betray Him. The imminent betrayal of Jesus is portrayed in two ways in the Gospel. There was the calculated and outright betrayal by Judas on one hand, and on the other, Peter's repeated denial of Jesus. The first, as the Gospel of John says, was buoyed by Satan, who entered unto Judas and egged him to do the deed. Peter's, though unplanned and unexpected, was nevertheless a manifestation of the weakness of his resolve, the weakness of his faith. This poignant scene marks the beginning of the events leading to the Cross, emphasizing the human struggles and choices that shape the unfolding drama.

Prayer:

Heavenly Father, on this Tuesday of Holy Week, we envision the unfolding drama of redemption. We recognize Jesus as the fulfillment of the prophetic mission, extending salvation to the ends of the earth. In the face of human frailty and betrayal, grant us the grace to trust in your deliverance and follow the example of Christ's humble obedience. Save us from the sins of disobedience and denial of your will. Through Christ our Lord. Amen.

Action for the Day:

1. Reflect on the universal mission of the suffering servant fulfilled in Jesus Christ.
2. Reflect on a time when you wished that you would have acted differently in a given situation. How could you have prepared yourself to be a stronger person?
3. Reflect on the choices made by Judas and Peter. How can you align your choices with a humble obedience to God's will?

Wednesday, March 27

Wednesday of Holy Week

First Reading: Isaiah 50:4-9a

Responsorial Psalm: Psalm 69:8-10, 21-22, 31 and 33-34

Gospel: Matthew 26:14-25

Reflection: The Suffering Servant and the Betrayal of Jesus

As Holy Week progresses, today's readings bring us into the profound mystery of the suffering servant and the foreboding betrayal by one of Jesus' closest disciples. The readings unveil the obedience of the Servant, the psalmist's cry for deliverance, and the tragic moment of betrayal at the Last Supper.

"The Lord GOD has given me a well-trained tongue, that I might know how to answer the weary a word that will waken them. Morning after morning he wakens my ear to hear as disciples do." - Isaiah 50:4

Isaiah's prophecy in the first reading, introduces the obedient Servant of the Lord, one who listens and speaks as instructed by God. This passage echoes Jesus' submission to the Father's will, setting the stage for the unfolding events leading to the Cross.

"For it is on your account I bear insult, that disgrace covers my face." - Psalm 69:8

The psalmist's words foreshadow the suffering and humiliation that the servant will endure, reflecting Jesus' experiences leading up to His crucifixion.

"He said in reply, 'He who has dipped his hand into the dish with me is the one who will betray me.'" - Matthew 26:23

In the Gospel of Matthew, Jesus reveals to His disciples that one of them will betray Him, a solemn moment that foreshadows the events of Maundy Thursday and Good Friday. Jesus recognizes that Judas is betraying him, but continues to place his total trust in God his Father. When Judas asks the chief priest, "What are you willing to give me if I hand him over to you?" it only means that his action is a sign of refusal to accept the Lord because his faith is weak. Doubt and greed of humans are signs of weaknesses of one's faith to turn away from the Lord. But God will always lead and guide our way back to the right path.

Prayer:

Heavenly Father, today, we reflect on the prophecies of the suffering servant in Isaiah and the somber revelation of Judas's betrayal of Jesus. We are reminded of the servant's mission to uplift the weary and the suffering that covers His face. Help us to offer words of comfort and hope to those in need. We also pray for the strength to resist the temptation to betray, whether through words or actions. May this reflection deepen our understanding of the sacrifices Jesus made for our redemption. Through Christ our Lord. Amen.

Action for the Day:

1. Reflect on the ways you can offer words of comfort and hope to those who are weary or suffering.
2. Consider the significance of loyalty and trust in your relationships and how you can strengthen them.
3. As Lent officially comes to an end tomorrow and the Mass of the Lord's Supper begins, reflect on your Lenten journey. How have you grown closer to God? How have you grown in holiness? Give thanks to God for accompanying you in this season.
4. Plan to participate in the liturgies of the Paschal Triduum in your parish from tomorrow.

Thursday, March 28

Holy Thursday

Chrism Mass

First Reading: Isaiah 61:1-3a, 6a, 8b-9

Responsorial Psalm: Psalm 89:21-22, 25 and 27

Second Reading: Revelation 1:5-8

Gospel: Luke 4:16-21

First Reading: Exodus 12:1-8, 11-14

Responsorial Psalm: Psalm 116:12-13, 15-16bc, 17-18.

Second Reading: 1 Corinthians 11:23-26

Gospel: John 13:1-15

Reflection: The Last Supper and the Gift of the Eucharist

On Holy Thursday, we begin the most sacred Triduum, the greatest feasts in the life of the Church. Today, we commemorate the Last Supper, a profound and sacred moment when Jesus instituted the Eucharist and washed the feet of His disciples. It is a day of deep significance as we envision the Passover Lamb whose blood brings redemption, lift the cup of salvation in gratitude, acknowledge the profound mystery of the Eucharist, and embrace the call to humble service exemplified by Jesus.

"This is how you are to eat it: with your loins girt, sandals on your feet and your staff in hand, you will eat it in a hurry. It is the LORD's Passover." - Exodus 12:11

In the first reading, we encounter the institution of the Passover, a crucial event in the history of Israel. God instructs the people to sacrifice a lamb and mark their doorposts with its blood. The blood serves as a sign of protection, foreshadowing the ultimate Lamb of God, Jesus Christ, whose blood redeems us from sin.

"I will raise the cup of salvation and call on the name of the LORD." - Psalm 116:13

The psalmist expresses gratitude for God's salvation, linking it to the cup of blessing and sacrifice. As we approach the Lord's

Supper, we join the psalmist in lifting the cup of salvation, acknowledging the precious gift of the Eucharist.

""This is my body that is for you. Do this in remembrance of me.""

- 1 Corinthians 11:24

In the second reading, Paul recounts the words of Jesus during the Last Supper, emphasizing the importance of the Eucharistic celebration. Reminding us that the Eucharist is not just a symbol but a true participation in the body and blood of Christ, thus drawing us into a profound communion with Him.

"I have given you a model to follow, so that as I have done for you, you should also do." - John 13:15

The Gospel narrative captures the powerful scene of Jesus washing the feet of His disciples, thus setting an example of service and profound humility for all His followers. Jesus, the Lord and Teacher, becomes a servant to His own, setting an enduring precedent for Christian discipleship.

Prayer:

Heavenly Father, on this Holy Thursday, we remember the Last Supper and the institution of the Eucharist, a gift of your abiding presence with us. We are grateful for the bread and wine that become the body and blood of Christ. As we receive this sacrament, may it nourish our souls and deepen our communion with Jesus. Help us to follow His example of humility and service, washing one another's feet in love. May the Eucharist be a source of unity and grace in our lives. Through Christ our Lord. Amen.

Action for the Day:

1. Attend a Holy Thursday Mass or service, where the

Eucharist is consecrated and the washing of feet may be reenacted.

2. Reflect on the profound gift of the Eucharist and how it deepens your relationship with Christ.

3. Consider ways in which you can imitate Jesus' example of humble service in your own life.

Friday, March 29

Good Friday of the Lord's Passion

First Reading: Isaiah 52:13-53:12

Responsorial Psalm: Psalm 31:2, 6, 12-13, 15-16, 17, 25

Second Reading: Hebrews 4:14-16; 5:7-9

Gospel: John 18:1-19:42

Reflection: The Crucifixion and the Sacrifice of Christ

Good Friday is a solemn and holy day when we commemorate the crucifixion and death of Jesus Christ. It is a day of profound reflection on the sacrifice He made for our redemption. It is observed during Holy Week as part of the Paschal Triduum. The Scripture readings invite us to contemplate the fulfillment of the prophecy of the Suffering Servant, the depth of Christ's sacrifice, and the profound impact of His death on our salvation.

"But he was pierced for our sins, crushed for our iniquity. He bore the punishment that makes us whole, by his wounds we were healed." - Isaiah 53:5

The prophecy of Isaiah in the first reading foretells the suffering and sacrifice of the Servant of the Lord who was pierced and crushed for our sins, emphasizing that through His wounds, we find healing. This passage poignantly describes the redemptive mission of Jesus, who bears our sins and offers Himself as a sacrificial lamb for the salvation of humanity.

"I trust in you, LORD; I say, 'You are my God.' My destiny is in your hands; rescue me from my enemies, from the hands of my pursuers. Let your face shine on your servant; save me in your mercy." - Psalm 31:15-17

The psalmist's cry expresses trust in God amid affliction and suffering. As we reflect on the events of Good Friday, this psalm becomes a prayer of solidarity with Christ, trusting in God's mercy and seeking refuge in His hands.

"Therefore, since we have a great high priest who has passed through the heavens, Jesus, the Son of God, let us hold fast to our confession." - Hebrews 4:14

The second reading reminds us that Jesus, our great high priest, sympathizes with our weaknesses and invites us to hold fast to our confession of faith.

The Gospel of John recounts the entirety of Jesus' passion, from His arrest in the Garden of Gethsemane to His crucifixion and burial. This narrative invites us to witness the depth of Jesus' love, obedience, and the ultimate sacrifice for the forgiveness of sins.

"'It is finished.' And bowing his head, he handed over the spirit." - John 19:30b

The final words of Jesus on the cross, entrusting His spirit to the Father, demonstrate His complete surrender to God's will and His sacrifice for our salvation.

Prayer:

Heavenly Father, on this Good Friday, we remember the profound sacrifice of Jesus on the cross. The words of Isaiah emphasize that His suffering was for our offenses and sins, and through His wounds, we find healing. We are moved by Jesus' surrender and entrusting of His spirit to you. As we reflect on His sacrifice, may we hold fast to our confession of faith and embrace the redemption He has secured for us. Through Christ our Lord. Amen.

Action for the Day:

1. Attend the Good Friday Mass, and participate in the veneration of the cross.
2. Spend time in quiet reflection and prayer, recalling the Lord's Passion. Pray the Stations of the Cross and reflect on Jesus' love expressed in his saving death.
3. Consider how you can live out your faith and confession in your daily actions, emulating Christ's love and sacrifice.

Saturday, March 30

Holy Saturday: At the Easter Vigil in the Holy Night of Easter

First Reading: Genesis 1:1-2:2 or 1:1, 26-31a

Responsorial Psalm: Psalm 104:1-2, 5-6, 10, 12, 13-14, 24, 35 or Psalm 33:4-5, 6-7, 12-13, 20 and 22

Second Reading: Genesis 22:1-18 or 22:1-2, 9a, 10-13, 15-18

Responsorial Psalm: Psalm 16:5, 8, 9-10, 11

Third Reading: Exodus 14:15-15:1

Responsorial Psalm: Exodus 15:1-2, 3-4, 5-6, 17-18

Fourth Reading: Isaiah 54:5-14

Responsorial Psalm: Psalm 30:2, 4, 5-6, 11-12, 13

Fifth Reading: Isaiah 55:1-11

Responsorial Psalm: Isaiah 12:2-3, 4, 5-6

Sixth Reading: Baruch 3:9-15, 32-4:4

Responsorial Psalm: Psalm 19:8, 9, 10, 11

Seventh Reading: Ezekiel 36:16-17a, 18-28

Responsorial Psalm: Psalm 42:3, 5; 43:3, 4

[When baptism is celebrated.]

Or:

Isaiah 12:2-3, 4bcd, 5-6 or Psalm 51:12-13, 14-15, 18-19

[When baptism is not celebrated.]

Epistle: Romans 6:3-11

Responsorial Psalm: Psalm 118:1-2, 16-17, 22-23

Gospel: Mark 16:1-7

Reflection: The Silence of Holy Saturday

Holy Saturday is a day of waiting, silence, and anticipation. It's a day when Jesus' body rests in the tomb, and the world holds its breath, awaiting the fulfillment of God's promises.

"And the earth was without form or shape, with darkness over the abyss and a mighty wind sweeping over the waters." -

Genesis 1:2

The first reading reminds us that God is the author of all life. In the creation narrative, we find the Spirit of God hovering over the formless and empty world, bringing life out of chaos. The Easter Vigil of Holy Saturday calls us to anticipate the new creation, inaugurated by Christ's resurrection, bringing forth a new humanity reconciled with God.

"I will give you a new heart, and a new spirit I will put within you. I will remove the heart of stone from your flesh and give you a heart of flesh." - Ezekiel 36:26

Ezekiel's prophecy speaks of God's promise to give His people a new heart and a new spirit, a promise that anticipates the resurrection and the transformation that comes through Christ's resurrection.

"We were indeed buried with him through baptism into death, so that, just as Christ was raised from the dead by the glory of the Father, we too might live in newness of life." - Romans 6:4

In the today's epistle, Paul in his letter to the Romans, underscores the profound meaning of baptism, where we die with Christ in order to rise with Him. This reading prepares us for the renewal of our baptismal promises during the Easter Vigil.

"He said to them, 'Do not be amazed! You seek Jesus of Nazareth, the crucified. He has been raised; he is not here. Behold, the place where they laid him.'" - Mark 16:6

The Gospel of Mark recounts the women discovering the empty tomb and the angel proclaiming the Resurrection. The Easter Vigil culminates in the joyous proclamation, "He has been raised!"

Prayer:

Heavenly Father, on this Holy Saturday, we embrace the silence and anticipation of this day. Just as the Spirit of God hovered over the waters in the Genesis account, we await the transformation and new life that your promises bring. We trust in the fulfillment of your Word, which gives us a new heart and a new spirit. Help us to remember that the silence of Holy Saturday is a prelude to the joy of Easter. As we wait in hope, may our hearts be prepared for the resurrection of Christ. Through Christ our Lord. Amen.

Action for the Day:

1. Embrace the silence and anticipation of Holy Saturday, setting aside time for quiet reflection and prayer.
2. Consider the promises of God in your life and how He has transformed your heart and spirit.
3. Plan to attend the Easter Vigil Mass and as you prepare for Easter, reflect on how well you have lived your Lenten promises during this journey.
4. Renew your baptismal promises and open your heart to the transformative power of Christ's resurrection.

Sunday, March 31

Easter Sunday: The Resurrection of the Lord

First Reading: Acts 10:34a, 37-43

Responsorial Psalm: Psalm 118:1-2, 16-17, 22-23.

Second Reading: Colossians 3:1-4 or 1 Corinthians 5:6b-8

Gospel: John 20:1-9

Reflection: The Triumph of Resurrection

Easter Sunday is the most joyful and celebratory day in the Christian calendar. On this day, we proclaim with great joy, *"Christ is risen!"* and celebrate the central event of our faith—the Resurrection of Jesus Christ. The readings invite us to ponder the universal impact of Christ's victory over death, the steadfast love of the Lord, the call to live a new life in Christ, and the mysterious emptiness of the tomb that proclaims the Resurrection. Let us renew our commitment to living in the joy of the Resurrection.

"This man God raised (on) the third day and granted that he be visible." - Acts 10:40

In the first reading from Acts of the Apostles, Peter proclaims the message of Jesus, emphasizing His death and resurrection. The resurrection is the cornerstone of our faith, bringing salvation to all who believe.

"By the LORD has this been done; it is wonderful in our eyes." - Psalm 118:23

The psalmist celebrates the Lord's steadfast love and the victory of His right hand. As we rejoice in the Resurrection, we echo the psalmist's proclamation that *"This is the day the LORD has made; let us rejoice in it and be glad." -* Psalm 118:24

"If then you were raised with Christ, seek what is above, where Christ is seated at the right hand of God." - Colossians 3:1

Or

"Therefore let us celebrate the feast, not with the old yeast, the yeast of malice and wickedness, but with the unleavened bread of sincerity and truth." - 1 Corinthians 5:8

The second reading of today is taken from either Colossians or Corinthians. In Colossians, Paul invites us to set our minds on things above, where Christ is seated at the right hand of God. While from the first letter to the Corinthians, Paul uses the imagery of unleavened bread to signify the sincerity and truth of the Christian life.

"When Simon Peter arrived after him, he went into the tomb and saw the burial cloths there, and the cloth that had covered his head, not with the burial cloths but rolled up in a separate place. Then the other disciple also went in, the one who had arrived at

the tomb first, and he saw and believed." - John 20:6-8

The Gospel of John recounts the discovery of the empty tomb by Mary of Magdala, Simon Peter and the other disciple whom Jesus loved. The absence of Jesus' body and the arrangement of the burial cloths point to the reality of the Resurrection. This passage captures the awe and wonder of that Easter morning.

The fulfillment of Jesus' promise of resurrection is a source of great hope and comfort, assuring us of the truth of His teachings.

Prayer:

Heavenly Father, on this glorious Easter Sunday, we celebrate the resurrection of your Son, Jesus Christ. The empty tomb is a powerful symbol of hope and victory over sin and death. We are filled with joy and gratitude for the promise of eternal life that His resurrection brings. As we proclaim, "Christ is risen," may this truth resonate in our hearts and lives. Thank you for the gift of salvation and the triumph of resurrection. Through Christ our Lord. Amen.

Action for the Day:

1. Attend an Easter Sunday Mass, and participate in the joyful celebration of Christ's resurrection.

2. Share the message of Christ's resurrection with friends and family, spreading the hope and joy of Easter.

3. Spend time in prayer, thanking God for the victory of resurrection and the promise of eternal life in Christ.

STATIONS OF THE CROSS

The presiding minister may be a priest, deacon, or layperson. This minister prays the opening and closing prayers, leads the acclamation, announces the stations, and says the prayer that concludes each station. One or more readers may read the Scriptural reflections. A period of silence should be observed between the Scripture reading and the prayer. A cross bearer accompanied by two candle bearers may stand in front of each station as it is announced.

Before Each Station

Minister: We adore you, O Christ, and we bless you.

All: Because by your holy cross you have redeemed the world.

After Each Station

All: Lord Jesus, help us walk in your steps.

Opening Prayer

Minister: God of power and mercy, in love you sent your Son that we might be cleansed of sin and live with you forever. Bless us as we gather to reflect on his suffering and death that we may learn from his example the way we should go. We ask this through that same Christ, our Lord.

All: Amen.

First Station: Jesus in the Garden of Gethsemane

Reader: Then Jesus came with them to a place called Gethsemane, and he said to his disciples, "Sit here while I go over there and pray." He took along Peter and the two sons of Zebedee, and began to feel sorrow and distress. Then he said to them, "My soul is sorrowful even to death. Remain here and keep watch with me." He advanced a little and fell prostrate in prayer, saying, "My Father, if it is possible, let this cup pass from me; yet, not as I will, but as you will." When he returned to his disciples he found them asleep. He said to Peter, "So you could not keep watch with me for one hour? Watch and pray that you may not undergo the test. The spirit is willing, but the flesh is weak."

(Matthew 26:36-41)

Minister: Lord, grant us your strength and wisdom, that we may seek to follow your will in all things

Second Station: Jesus, Betrayed by Judas, is Arrested

Reader: Then, while [Jesus] was still speaking, Judas, one of the Twelve, arrived, accompanied by a crowd with swords and clubs, who had come from the chief priests, the scribes, and the elders. His betrayer had arranged a signal with them, saying, "The man I shall kiss is the one; arrest him and lead him away securely." He came and immediately went over to him and said, "Rabbi." And he kissed him. At this they laid hands on him and arrested him.

(Mark 14: 43-46)

Minister: Lord, grant us the courage of our convictions that our lives may faithfully reflect the good news you bring.

Third Station: Jesus Is Condemned By the Sanhedrin

Reader: When day came the council of elders of the people met, both chief priests and scribes, and they brought him before their Sanhedrin. They said, "If you are the Messiah, tell us," but he replied to them, "If I tell you, you will not believe, and if I question, you will not respond. But from this time on the Son of Man will be seated at the right hand of the power of God." They all asked, "Are you then the Son of God?" He replied to them, "You say that I am." Then they said, "What further need have we for testimony? We have heard it from his own mouth."

(Luke 22: 66-71)

Minister: Lord, grant us your sense of righteousness that we may never cease to work to bring about the justice of the kingdom that you promised.

Fourth Station: Jesus Is Denied By Peter

Reader: Now Peter was sitting outside in the courtyard. One of the maids came over to him and said, "You too were with Jesus the Galilean." But he denied it in front of everyone, saying, "I do not know what you are talking about!" As he went out to the gate, another girl saw him and said to those who were there, "This man was with Jesus the Nazorean." Again he denied it with an oath, "I do not know the man!" A little later the bystanders came over and said to Peter, "Surely you too are one of them; even your speech gives you away." At that he began to curse and to swear, "I do not know the man." And immediately a cock crowed. Then Peter remembered the word that Jesus had spoken: "Before the cock crows you will deny me three times." He went out and began to weep bitterly.

(Matthew 26: 69-75)

Minister: Lord, grant us the gift of honesty that we may not fear to speak the truth even when difficult.

Fifth Station: Jesus Is Judged By Pilate

Reader: The chief priests with the elders and the scribes, that is, the whole Sanhedrin, held a council. They bound Jesus, led him away, and handed him over to Pilate. Pilate questioned him, "Are you the king of the Jews?" He said to him in reply, "You say so." The chief priests accused him of many things. Again Pilate questioned him, "Have you no answer? See how many things they accuse you of." Jesus gave him no further answer, so that Pilate was amazed. —Pilate, wishing to satisfy the crowd, released Barrabas— [and] handed [Jesus] over to be crucified.
(Mark 15: 1-5, 15)

Minister: Lord, grant us discernment that we may see as you see, not as the world sees.

Sixth Station: Jesus is Scourged and Crowned with Thorns

Reader: Then Pilate took Jesus and had him scourged. And the soldiers wove a crown out of thorns and placed it on his head, and clothed him in a purple cloak, and they came to him and said, "Hail, King of the Jews!" And they struck him repeatedly.
(John 19: 1-3)

Minister: Lord, grant us patience in times of suffering that we may offer our lives as a sacrifice of praise.

Seventh Station: Jesus Bears The Cross

Reader: When the chief priests and the guards saw [Jesus] they cried out, "Crucify him, crucify him!" Pilate said to them, "Take him yourselves and crucify him. I find no guilt in him." They cried out, "Take him away, take him away! Crucify him!" Pilate said to them, "Shall I crucify your king?" The chief priests answered, "We have no king but Caesar." Then he handed him over to them to be crucified. So they took Jesus, and carrying the cross himself he went out to what is called the Place of the Skull, in Hebrew, Golgotha.

(John 19: 6, 15-17)

Minister: Lord, grant us strength of purpose that we may faithfully bear our crosses each day.

Eighth Station: Jesus Is Helped By Simon the Cyrenian to Carry The Cross

Reader: They pressed into service a passer-by, Simon, a Cyrenian, who was coming in from the country, the father of Alexander and Rufus, to carry his cross.

(Mark 15: 21)

Minister: Lord, grant us willing spirits that we may be your instruments on earth.

Ninth Station: Jesus Meets the Women of Jerusalem

Reader: A large crowd of people followed Jesus, including many women who mourned and lamented him. Jesus turned to them and said, "Daughters of Jerusalem, do not weep for me; weep instead for yourselves and for your children, for indeed, the days are coming when people will say, 'Blessed are the barren, the wombs that never bore and the breasts that never nursed.' At that time, people will say to the mountains, 'Fall upon us!' and to the hills, 'Cover us!' for if these things are done when the wood is green what will happen when it is dry?"

(Luke 23: 27-31)

Minister: Lord, grant us gentle spirits that we may comfort those who mourn.

Tenth Station: Jesus Is Crucified

Reader: When they came to the place called the Skull, they crucified him and the criminals there, one on his right, the other on his left. [Then Jesus said, "Father, forgive them, they know not what they do."]

(Luke 23: 33-34)

Minister: Lord, grant us merciful hearts that we may bring your reconciliation and forgiveness to all.

Eleventh Station: Jesus Promises His Kingdom to the Good Thief

Reader: Now one of the criminals hanging there reviled Jesus, saying, "Are you not the Messiah? Save yourself and us." The other, however, rebuking him, said in reply, "Have you no fear of God, for you are subject to the same condemnation? And indeed, we have been condemned justly, for the sentence we received corresponds to our crimes, but this man has done nothing criminal." Then he said, "Jesus, remember me when you come into your kingdom." He replied to him, "Amen, I say to you, today you will be with me in Paradise."

(Luke 23: 39-43)

Minister: Lord, grant us perseverance that we may never stop seeking you.

Twelfth Station: Jesus Speaks To His Mother and the Disciple

Reader: Standing by the cross of Jesus were his mother and his mother's sister, Mary the wife of Clopas, and Mary of Magdala. When Jesus saw his mother and the disciple there whom he loved, he said to his mother, "Woman, behold, your son." Then he said to the disciple, "Behold, your mother." And from that hour the disciple took her into his home.
(John 19: 25-27)

Minister: Lord, grant us constancy that we may be willing to stand by those in need.

Thirteenth Station: Jesus Dies on the Cross

Reader: It was now about noon and darkness came over the whole land until three in the afternoon because of an eclipse of the sun. Then the veil of the temple was torn down the middle. Jesus cried out in a loud voice, "Father, into your hands I commend my spirit"; and when he had said this he breathed his last.
(Luke 23: 44-46)

Minister: Lord, grant us trust in you that when our time on earth in ended our spirits may come to you without delay.

Fourteenth Station: Jesus Is Placed in the Tomb

Reader: When it was evening, there came a rich man from Arimathea named Joseph, who was himself a disciple of Jesus. He went to Pilate and asked for the body of Jesus; then Pilate ordered it to be handed over. Taking the body, Joseph wrapped it [in] clean linen and laid it in his new tomb that he had hewn in the rock. Then he rolled a huge stone across the entrance to the tomb and departed.

(Matthew 27: 57-60)

Minister: Lord, grant us your compassion that we may always provide for those in need.

Closing Prayer

Minister: Lord Jesus Christ, your passion and death is the sacrifice that unites earth and heaven and reconciles all people to you. May we who have faithfully reflected on these mysteries follow in your steps and so come to share your glory in heaven where you live and reign with the Father and the Holy Spirit one God, forever and ever.

All: Amen.

SACRAMENT OF PENANCE

The Sacrament of Penance is one of the seven sacraments of the Catholic Church, in which Catholics who have sinned but moved by the Holy Spirit obtain forgiveness from the mercy of God for sins committed after baptism. This sacrament is granted through the priest's absolution to those who with true sorrow, confess their sins and promise to satisfy for the same. Not only does it [the Sacrament of Penance] free us from our sins but it also challenges us to have the same kind of compassion and forgiveness for those who sin against us.

It is strongly recommended as a penitential practice during the entire Lenten Season. Moreover, Catholics are obliged to confess before receiving Holy Communion during the Easter season. It offers us a great opportunity to experience God's boundless mercy and also an encounter with Jesus Christ, who after rising from the dead breathed the Holy Spirit on his Apostles— the first priests— and gave them the power to forgive sins in his name (John 20:23)

Examination of Conscience

An Examination of Conscience is helpful in preparing for confessing one's sins in the sacrament of Penance. It helps one to reflect prayerfully over several areas of one's life to identify any sins committed against God through one's actions, thoughts, words, and even inaction. This done before approaching the Priest in Confession by setting aside some quiet time for reflection. This will help you call to mind your sins and failings.

We hope you find any of the following types of examinations of conscience useful in preparing for confession.

Examination of Conscience based on the Ten Commandments

First Commandment

I am the LORD your God. You shall worship the Lord your God and Him only shall you serve.

Have I...

- Reserved or harbored hatred for God?
- Disobeyed the commandments of God or the Church?
- Refused to accept what God has revealed as true, or what the Catholic Church proclaims for belief?
- Denied the existence of God?
- Neglected to nourish and protect my faith?
- Deliberately misled others about doctrine or the faith?
- Rejected the Catholic faith, joined another Christian denomination, or joined or practiced another religion?
- Joined a group forbidden to Catholics (Masons, communists, etc.)?
- Despaired about my salvation or the forgiveness of my sins?
- Presumed God's mercy? (Committing a sin in expectation of forgiveness, or asking for forgiveness without interior conversion and practicing virtue.)
- Loved someone or something more than God (money, power, sex, ambition, etc.)?
- Let someone or something influence my choices more than God?
- Engaged in superstitious practices? (Including horoscopes, fortune tellers, etc.)

- Been involved in the occult or occult practices?
- Formally attempted to leave the Catholic Church?
- Hidden a serious sin or told a lie in Confession?

Second Commandment

You shall not take the name of the Lord your God in vain.

Have I...

- Used the name of God in cursing or blasphemy?
- Failed to keep vows, promises, or resolutions that I have made to God? [specify in the confessional which one; the Priest has authority to remove the obligations of promises and resolutions if they are too rash or unjust]
- Spoken about the Faith, the Church, the saints, or sacred things with irreverence, hatred or defiance?
- Watched television or movies, or listened to music that treated God, the Church, the saints, or sacred things irreverently?
- Used vulgar, suggestive or obscene speech?
- Belittled others in my speech?
- Behaved disrespectfully in the church building (e.g., *talking immoderately in church* before, during, or after holy Mass)?
- Misused places or things set apart for the worship of God?
- Committed perjury? (Breaking an oath or lying under oath.)
- Blamed God for my failings?

Third Commandment

Remember to keep holy the Sabbath day.

Have I...

- Missed Mass on Sunday or Holy Days (through own fault without sufficient reason)?
- Neglected to set time aside each day for personal prayer to God?
- Committed a sacrilege against the Blessed Sacrament (thrown Him away; brought Him home; treated Him carelessly, etc.)?
- Received any sacrament while in the state of mortal sin?
- Habitually come late to and/or leave early from Mass?
- Shop, labor, practice sports or do business unnecessarily on Sunday or other Holy Days of Obligation?
- Not attended to taking my children to Mass?
- Not provided proper instruction in the Faith to my children?
- Knowingly eaten meat on a forbidden day (or not fasted on a fast day)?
- Eaten or drunken within one hour of receiving Communion (other than medical need)?

Fourth Commandment

Honor your father and your mother.

Have I...

- (*If still under my parents' care*) Obeyed all that my parents reasonably asked of me?
- Shown disregard for my parents' wishes, displayed contempt of their demands, and/or disdained their very

being?

- Neglected the needs of my parents in their old age or in their time of need?
- Harbored hatred for my parents?
- Brought shame on them?
- (*If still in school*) Obeyed the reasonable demands of my teachers?
- Disrespected my teachers?
- (*If I have children*) Neglected to give my children proper food, clothing, shelter, education, discipline and care (even after Confirmation)?
- Provided for the religious education and formation of my children for as long as they are under my care?
- Ensured that my children still under my care regularly frequent the sacraments of Penance and Holy Communion?
- Educated my children in a way that corresponds to Catholic religious disciplines?
- Provided my children with a positive, prudent and personalized education in the Catholic teaching on human sexuality?
- Been to my children a good example of how to live the Catholic Faith?
- Prayed with and for my children?
- (*for everyone*) Lived in humble obedience to those who legitimately exercise authority over me?
- Broken any just law?
- Supported or voted for a politician whose positions are

opposed to the teachings of Christ and the Catholic Church?

- Failed to pray for the deceased members of my family— the Poor Souls of Purgatory included?

Fifth Commandment

You shall not murder.

Have I...

- Unjustly and intentionally killed a human being (murder)?
- Have I been guilty, through negligence and/or lacking of intention, of the death of another (killing)?
- Been involved in an abortion, directly or indirectly (through advice, encouragement, providing money, or facilitating it in any other way)?
- Seriously considered or attempted suicide?
- Supported, promoted, or encouraged the practice of assisted suicide or mercy killing (euthanasia)?
- Deliberately desired to kill an innocent human being?
- Unjustly inflicted bodily harm on another person?
- Unjustly threatened another person with bodily harm?
- Verbally or emotionally abused another person?
- Gossiped, slandered, detracted, calumniated?
- Hated another person, or wished him/her evil?
- Been prejudiced, or unjustly discriminated against others because of their race, color, nationality, sex or religion?
- Joined a hate group?
- Purposely provoked another by teasing or nagging?
- Recklessly endangered my life or health, or that of another,

by my actions?

- Driven recklessly or under the influence of alcohol or other drugs?
- Abused alcohol or other drugs?
- Sold or given drugs to others to use for non-therapeutic purposes?
- Used tobacco immoderately?
- Over-eaten?
- Encouraged others to sin by giving scandal?
- Helped another to commit a mortal sin (through advice, driving them somewhere, dressing and/or acting immodestly, etc.)?
- Caused serious injury of another by criminal neglect?
- Indulged in unjust anger?
- Refused to control my temper?
- Been fateful to, quarreled with, or willfully hurt someone?
- Been unforgiving of others, especially when mercy or pardon was requested?
- Sought revenge or hoped something bad would happen to someone?
- Delighted to see someone else get hurt or suffer?
- Treated animals cruelly, causing them to suffer or die needlessly?

Sixth & Ninth Commandments

You shall not commit adultery.

You shall not covet your neighbor's wife.

Have I...

- Neglected to practice and grow in the virtue of chastity?
- Given in to lust? (The desire for sexual pleasure unrelated to spousal love in marriage.)
- Used an artificial means of birth control (including withdrawal)?
- Refused to be open to conception, without just cause? (Catechism, 2368)
- Participated in immoral techniques such as in vitro fertilization or artificial insemination?
- Sterilized my sex organs for contraceptive purposes?
- Deprived my spouse of the marital right, without just cause?
- Claimed my own marital right without concern for my spouse?
- Deliberately caused male climax outside of normal sexual intercourse?
- Masturbated? (Deliberate stimulation of one's own sexual organs for sexual pleasure outside of the conjugal act.) (Catechism, 2366)
- Willfully entertained impure thoughts?
- Purchased, viewed, or made use of pornography?
- Watched or promoted movies and television that involve sex and nudity?
- Listened to music or jokes that are harmful to purity?
- Read books that are immoral?
- Committed adultery? (Sexual relations with someone who is married, or with someone other than my spouse.)
- Committed incest? (Sexual relations with a relative closer

than the third degree or an in-law.)

- Committed fornication? (Sexual relations with someone of the opposite sex when the two are not married to one another or any others.)
- Engaged in homosexual activity? (Sexual activity with someone of the same sex)
- Committed rape?
- Engaged in sexual foreplay (e.g., "petting", or excessive touching) reserved for marriage?
- Preyed upon children or youth for my sexual pleasure (pedophilia)?
- Engaged in unnatural sexual activities (anything that is not inherently natural to the sexual act; e.g., sex toys, even in the context of marriage)?
- Engaged in prostitution, or paid for the services of a prostitute?
- Seduced someone, or allowed myself to be seduced?
- Made uninvited and unwelcome sexual advances toward another?
- Purposely dressed immodestly?

Seventh & Tenth Commandments

You shall not steal.

You shall not covet your neighbor's goods.

Have I...

- Stolen? (Taken something that doesn't belong to me against the reasonable will of the owner.)
- Envied others on account of their possessions?

- Neglected to live in a spirit of Gospel poverty and simplicity?
- Neglected to give generously to others in need?
- Not considered that God has provided me with money so that I might use it to benefit others, as well as for my own legitimate needs?
- Neglected to practice the corporal works of mercy?
- Deliberately defaced, destroyed or lost another's property?
- Cheated on a test, taxes, sports, games, or in business?
- Squandered money in compulsive gambling?
- Make a false claim to an insurance company?
- Paid my employees a living wage, or failed to give a full day's work for a full day's pay?
- Failed to honor my part of a contract?
- Failed to make good on a debt?
- Overcharge someone, especially to take advantage of another's hardship or ignorance?
- Misused natural resources?

Eighth Commandment

You shall not bear false witness against your neighbor.

Have I...

- Lied?
- Knowingly and willfully deceived another?
- Perjured myself under oath?
- Gossiped?
- Committed detraction? (Destroying a person's reputation by telling others about his faults for no good reason.)

- Committed slander or calumny? (Telling lies about another person in order to destroy his reputation.)
- Committed libel? (Writing lies about another person in order to destroy his reputation. Libel is in substance different from slander because the written word has a longer "life" of damage)
- Been guilty of rash judgment? (Assuming the worst of another person based on circumstantial evidence.)
- Failed to make reparation for a lie I told, or for harm done to a person's reputation?
- Failed to speak out in defense of the Catholic Faith, the Church, or of another person?
- Betrayed another's confidence through speech, deed, or in writing?

Examination of Conscience based on the Precepts of the Church

First Precept of the Church

You shall attend Mass on Sundays and Holy from servile labor.

- (see Third Commandment above)

Second Precept of the Church

You shall confess your sins (to a Priest) at least once a year.

Have I...

- Made a good Confession of my mortal sins at least once a year?
- Purposely omitted telling my mortal sins in my last Confession?

- Neglected to perform the penance I was given?
- Neglected to make reparation for any harm I have done to others?

Third Precept of the Church

You shall receive the Sacrament of the Holy Eucharist at least during the Easter season.

Have I...

- Neglected to fulfill my Easter duty to receive Holy Communion at least once between the First Sunday of Lent and Trinity Sunday?
- Received Holy Communion while in the state of mortal sin?
- Failed to fast for at least one hour before receiving Holy Communion?
- Received Holy Communion more than twice in one day?

Fourth Precept of the Church

You shall observe the days of fasting and abstinence established by the Church.

Have I...

- Neglected to do *penance every Friday of the year*, if *not* abstaining from meat?
- Neglected to *abstain* from meat on Ash Wednesday and the Fridays of Lent (*if I am 14 years of age and/or older*)?
- Neglected to *fast* on Ash Wednesday and Good Friday (*if I am between the ages of 18 and 59*)?
- Neglected to spend time in prayer, do spiritual and

corporal works of mercy, and practice self-denial?

Fifth Precept of the Church

You shall help to provide for the needs of the Church.

Have I...

- Neglected to contribute a just amount of my time, talents and money to support my parish and the work of the Church?
- Neglected to support the Church by not trying to become a saint or by not striving to make sincere progress each day in sanctity?

Confession

Confession brings reconciliation between God and the penitent (person confessing his sins), between the penitent and others, and to the individual penitent. Confession presumes the penitent is truly sorry with a firm resolve not to sin again.

Guide to Making a Good Confession

Here is a guide to making a good confession.

(*Note: Penitent: the person confessing his sins and Confessor: the Priest administering the Sacrament.*)

1. The Penitent enters the confessional and kneels down at the screen. Depending on the confessional, you may either kneel or sit.

2. The Penitent, making the sign of the cross, says, "***Bless me, Father, for I have sinned. It has been*** _____ (state how many days, weeks, months, or years) *** since my last confession. These are my sins.***"

3. The Penitent confesses his sins. It might be helpful to start with the one that is most difficult to say since it will make it easier to mention the rest. The Confessor listens, but he may ask questions if something the Penitent has said is unclear or in order to lead the Penitent to a more thorough examination of conscience. *(Remember that for a confession to be valid, all mortal sins— each **kind** and the **number** of times committed —**must** be confessed. All venial sins **should** be confessed.)*

4. When the Penitent finishes confessing, he signifies this by saying: ***"For these and all the sins of my past, I am truly sorry."*** The Confessor may offer some advice or counsel, so that the Penitent may take the necessary steps to amend his life.

5. The Confessor then gives a penance (usually a prayer or a good work) which the penitent must do on leaving the confessional.

6. After giving the penance, the Confessor then instructs the Penitent to say an Act of Contrition.

7. After saying the Act of Contrition, the Confessor prays the prayer of Absolution (forgiveness). Listen attentively to that prayer, bless yourself as he makes the Sign of the Cross and at the end of the prayer, answer, ***"Amen."***

8. The Confessor will say, ***"Give thanks to the Lord for He is good."*** at which the Penitent responds, ***"His mercy endures forever."*** The Confessor then concludes by saying, ***"Your sins are forgiven. Go in peace."*** and the Penitent responds, ***"Thanks be to God."***

9. The Penitent leaves the confessional thanking God for the

sacrament just received and perform the penance as soon as possible.

Contrition

The Holy Catholic Church teaches that without sorrow for sin there is no forgiveness. Hence Contrition (or inner conversion of heart), which holds the first place among the acts of the penitent, is defined as "sorrow of heart and detestation for sin committed, together with the resolution not to sin again."

The prayer of penance that is prayed after confessing one's sins to a priest in confession is known as the *Act of Contrition*. After making an act of contrition, the priest will grant absolution to the penitent, absolving him/her of their sins by the grace of God.

There are a variety of different *Acts of Contrition* suggested in the Sacrament of Penance. Here are a few of them.

Act of Contrition (traditional)

O my God,

I am heartily sorry for having offended Thee,

and I detest all my sins,

because I dread the loss of heaven, and the pains of hell;

but most of all because they offend Thee, my God,

Who are all good and deserving of all my love.

I firmly resolve, with the help of Thy grace,

to confess my sins, to do penance,

and to amend my life. Amen.

Act of Contrition (alternate form)

My God, I am sorry for my sins with all my heart.

In choosing to do wrong and failing to do good,

I have sinned against you whom I should love above all things.

I firmly intend, with your help, to do penance, to sin no more, and

to avoid whatever leads me to sin.

Our Savior Jesus Christ suffered and died for us.

In his name, my God, have mercy. Amen

An Act of Contrition inspired by the Gospels

Father of mercy,

like the prodigal son

I return to you and say:

"I have sinned against you

and am no longer worthy to be called your son."

Christ Jesus, Savior of the world,

I pray with the repentant thief

to whom you promised Paradise:

"Lord, remember me in your kingdom."

Holy Spirit, fountain of love,

I call on you with trust:

"Purify my heart,

and help me to walk as a child of light." Amen

An Act of Contrition inspired by the Gospels

Lord Jesus,

you opened the eyes of the blind,

healed the sick,

forgave the sinful woman,

and after Peter's denial confirmed him in your love.

Listen to my prayer:

forgive all my sins,

renew your love in my heart,

help me to live in perfect unity with my fellow Christians

that I may proclaim your saving power to all the world. Amen

An Act of Contrition inspired by Psalm 51

Lord God,

in your goodness have mercy on me:

do not look on my sins,

but take away all my guilt.

Create in me a clean heart

and renew within me an upright spirit. Amen

Act of Contrition inspired by Psalm 24:6-7

Remember, Lord, your compassion and mercy

which you showed long ago.

Do not recall the sins and failings of my youth.

In your mercy remember me, Lord, because of your goodness.

Amen

An Act of Contrition to Our Lord Jesus

Lord Jesus,

you chose to be called the friend of sinners.

By your saving death and resurrection

free me from my sins.

May your peace take root in my heart

and bring forth a harvest

of love, holiness, and truth. Amen

An Act of Contrition to Jesus, the Lamb of God

Lord Jesus Christ,

you are the Lamb of God;

you take away the sins of the world.

Through the grace of the Holy Spirit

restore me to friendship with your Father,

cleanse me from every stain of sin

in the blood you shed for me,

and raise me to new life

for the glory of your name. Amen

Act of Contrition inspired by the Prayer of Jesus

Lord Jesus, Son of God,

have mercy on me, a sinner. Amen

Made in the USA
Coppell, TX
14 February 2024

29000020R10075